ISBN 978-0-483-02661-2
PIBN 10788046

FIVE POEMS.

BY

J. J. RIPLEY, ESQ.

LONDON:

PRINTED BY CHARLES AND EDWIN LAYTON,

150, FLEET STREET.

1855.

WEST END, HAMPSTEAD,

1855.

I request my friends to receive with indulgence the five following Poems, principally composed, long since, in my daily walks between Home and Office, and now printed for distribution among them, as a token of my regard.

The four first in order have little other pretension than an attempt to ornament by versification the popular stories on which they are founded. The fifth—a Poem of higher and more solemn character than it became me to undertake—with little better claim than those which precede it, has, I am sensible, need of far greater indulgence.

J. J. RIPLEY.

CONTENTS.

Reculver:

A LEGEND OF THE SISTERS.

INTRODUCTION.

My guide awaits me; nor do I refuse [1]
  With thee to leave awhile the loveliest home—
The fragrant flower plots of many hues;
  The vine bunch glassy; the nectareous pome;
The chestnut's thick and now most grateful shade;
  The oaks, which, branching to thy portal, wear
  The majesty of many a hundred year,
Amid the lessening land in thine own groves arrayed.

The hill declines, and we have said adieu;
  Yet mindful of a sometime shaded hour,
When the brown upland rising, to our view
  But just permitted, hides the village tower—
Sacred too soon to the departed guest [2]
  Who knows thy hospitality no more,
  Yet owns thy sepulchre, his sojourn o'er,
As in Samaria by the prophet laid to rest. [3]

We pass not, till his requiem is sung,
  The level valley whither Stour retires
Between the slopes with wood or verdure hung
  From Cantuaria's faintly pictured spires.
Our gentle steeds obey the rein and hand
  Which find them footing on a pass untried, [4]
  And lightly buoyant on the trembling tide;
Then pause on Thanet's soil; then bear us from the strand.

B

And, last, the confines of the isle are gained,
    Extending in primeval solitude;
Where yet the sunshine and sea breeze have reigned,
    In freshness and in fervour unsubdued.
The corn is gathered, and the landmark rare;
    Thinly the tree, the fold and dwelling, strown—
    But somewhat like an echo of renown
Amid the calm awakes, and seems repeated there.

Hist we the nearer sounding of the surge
    Those beaten and defenceless shores among.
Yon cliff, abrupt upon the wat'ry verge—
    Where is the plain which once it overhung;
A vestige that Severus' castle stood,[5]
    The royal house of Ethelbert; the bower
    By Eadred given to be a saintly dower—
Where is their place?　Alas! a place beneath the flood.

Upon the broken sand where ocean basks
    Smooth in oblivion of the wintry storm,
Some careful peasants urge in vain the tasks,
    Such as their skill and labour may perform,
To shield their margin from the billows' sweep:
    In range oblique the heavy piles are fixed,
    Bound, and with pliant brushwood intermixed,
To baffle or elude the mighty refluent deep.

Yet has Reculver's venerable fane[6]
    Its station on the relics of the land:
Between the Sister Towers, which yet remain,
    The fretted arch and pediment expand;
And pious care has perfected anew
    The stately form of each ascending spire,
    Which yet may warn the pilot to retire
Ere on the perilous shoal he dash his homebound crew.

Its ancient walls protect the holy place,
   And pavement, laid with obsolete device;
Though roofless those, and tott'ring to their base,
   And this bereft of many-coloured dyes;
And though the tomb retain no kingly dust;
    While bones, which mouldered in the mother soil,
    Amid the wreck disclosed, are ocean's spoil:
For here the grave, sea-worn, has rendered up its trust.

Perhaps, of those who labour on the beach
   To guard or to redeem their heritage,
There are who pause amid their toil, and teach
   The progress of its foe from age to age;
And gentle strangers, who have wandered here,
    May listen to a legend of the deep
    Which sometime made Reculver's rudest weep—
Which thus the bard repeats: and who disdain to hear?

PART I.

The sunbeams brightened over many a cloud,
   Seaward propelled by light ambrosial gale,
That, wending with the halcyon tide, allowed
   An easy progress to the distant sail,
Which seemed beneath the light and shade to veer,
   Averted from Reculver's holy strand,
   And little heeded of a rustic band
Who viewed it bounding by upon its blithe career.

They saw the shadow and the ray succeed,
   Without a thought on their vicissitude,
And gaily bade the gliding vessel speed.
   But, with the waning of the hour, more rude
The breeze, the billow less auspicious grew.
   Then apprehensions of the crowd awoke;
   Of their deceitful sands in doubt they spoke,
And trusted to their saints the safety of the crew.

Whate'er they whispered, or, perchance, expressed,
   To one who travelled on their path alone,
His gentle tidings thus awhile repressed:
   "St. Benedict is gracious to his own.
He, with good angels, has that bark in care:
   It holds, methinks, a mother of his house,
   Gone forth from Faversham to pay her vows
At Bradstowe's sea-girt shrine—the Lady of St. Clair.

" A calmer spirit and more spotless mind
   Ne'er bade the vanities of life farewell—
Too tender for the world which she resigned—
   Protected, but not hidden, in her cell :
While men, a multitude whom feudal awe
   Held hardly patient of her sire's command,
   Revere the rule in her monastic hand,
And zealously obey the meek Superior's law.

" Religious rite, and charitable care,
   And occupations such as these allow—
An orphan sister, Isabel St. Clair,
   Not long a sweet associate in her vow—
Have busied her for thrice five summers' tide.
   One love is theirs to whom one hour gave birth ;
   And, since bright Isabel was weaned from earth,
They pass the livelong day secluded side by side.

" We had beheld the holy mother pale
   With sickness such as heaven has removed ;
And she will keep the new May festival
   Within that chapel of the Virgin loved [7]
And graced by miracles and cures divine,
   Which, when the mariner returning sees,
   He slackens sail before a fav'ring breeze,
And strikes his topmost low in honour of the shrine.

" I heard the noontide bell o'er Medway toll,
   Amid the gratulations of the poor ;
And those who had distributed the dole
   Hardly repressed them from th' expanding door
Which gave the van of the procession way :
   I saw the breath of fuming censers toss,
   In honour of th' Invention of the Cross,[8]
And unshod palmers bare bring on the meek array.

" Lay sisters after—then those unprofessed,
    Who keep noviciate in the convent's aisle,
White-robed, with hands composed upon the breast,
    And eyes as yet unguarded by the veil.
The symphony, which sank awhile, confined
    Beneath the brows of the repellent arch,
    Broke forth anon, amid the lengthened march,
And words of holy song were borne upon the wind.

" Then—in its most triumphant measure loud,
    When after solemn pause and interval,
Proceeded, to the Saint of Broadstowe vowed,
    A golden reliquary, wrapped in pall.
The grey-robed almoner of high St. Clair,
    By six accompanied, succeeding six
    Who joined to bear a silver crucifix,
Displayed the gorgeous gift, and said appointed prayer.

" The pious multitude had bowed the knee,
    And kept unbroken silence while they came ;
Then fell in whispers, ' Benedicite,'
    And awe and stillness ceased in glad acclaim:
For then the bounteous mother met their gaze.
    She lifted up her meek eyes from the ground,
    And, ere they fell upon her friends around,
Collected holy thoughts, and gave her saint the praise.

" Her elder sisters hastened to sustain
    Her yet unequal steps, with duteous pride ;
The younger Benedictines filled her train—
    All in their solemn weeds of wool undyed,[9]
And sable stole, and hood, and scapular.
    So forth they went along the flow'r-strewn way,
    And parted on the margin of the bay,
With chorus and response flung faintly from afar—

Chorus.

" ' Beloved saint, in thy protection have
Those that are left the keepers of thy door ! '

Response.

" ' All those of thine that occupy the wave,
To thy blest courts, beloved saint, restore ! '

" Such was the strain—while to the rippling tide
The lady hastened, with a chosen few;
And those divided, while they signed adieu,
Unwillingly retired, and often turned aside."

Reculver's sons around the speaker pressed.
Some, with the grave garrulity of age,
The Lady's name and holy office blessed,
And praised the purpose of her pilgrimage.
The younger comments light and briefly ran,
And many quitted and rejoined the throng
With frequent tribute of an idle tongue,
And all forget th' alarm wherewith their speech began.

Yet had the darkness gathered while they spoke,
And once the barbéd lightning flashed amain;
Then, instantaneously, loud thunder broke;
And pattered ever and anon deep rain,
Fitfully tossed upon the whirling wind,
Which met the tide where Thames and Swale unite,[10]
Lashed into fury by its opposite;
And distant ocean howled, and cheerless day declined.

Amid the darkness o'er th' horizon hung,
   And flash and peal, filled faster and more fast,
Where is the bark?   Upon the quicksands flung,
   Or, peradventure, driv'n before the blast.
The gazers see it not—their spirits sink;
   And while they shudder for the tempest-tossed,
   In fond and vain imaginations lost,
This seems surpassing hope, and that too sad to think.

They listened, and their ear received no sound
   Save of the hurricane, and billows' dash.
They left their shelter-place, and looked around
   On ocean, as it drank th' electric flash.
Twice after midnight waned the hour—the storm
   Sank, and the weariest gave themselves to sleep:
   When voice and whistle issued from the deep,
And, where the lightning died, emerged a dusky form.

The watchful, with a loud tumultuous cry
   Aroused the slumberers, and sprang to aid;
All that their haste for rescue could supply,
   Flung to the shoulder, in the hand displayed.
Their torches glanced upon the ruddy sand;
   In every wind arose a nearer call,
   A seaman's voice at every interval.
The form escaped the surge, and lay upon the land—

A shattered bark, which yet in safety held
   All that had trusted to its fragile plank,
When, in severe extremity, compelled
   To leave their vessel, sand-locked, ere she sank.
A female garment fluttered here and there
   Among the weary men who dropped the oar;
   And, by the first that struggled to the shore,
Was reverently borne the Lady of St. Clair.

In silence she submitted to their aid—
   The prompt humanities of those around;
Until her almoner, approaching, said,
   " Lo, lady! we were lost, and have been found [11]
Through him who laboured thus a night and day "
   (He pointed to an image on his cope).
   " Father! how found? she perishes, past hope,"
The sufferer replied; and sank, and died away.

And Heaven, most indulgent in her woes,
   Permitted her unconsciousness of all,
Until the melancholy morning rose,
   And seaward rang the ready boatman's call.
With many of the rescued in his crew,
   He made the wreck, impatient to bear
   Escape to such as were surviving there;
And set his curving sail, and vanished from the view.

PART II.

YET with the promise of a happier dawn,
　The Lady of St. Clair and Isabel
Had seen their yester solitude withdrawn,
　And looked upon a world which pleased them well,
And found the freedom ne'er so sweet before.
　They joyed in every living thing that stirred;
　In each new sound a gratulation heard;
With placid, pious thoughts, on one sad trial o'er.

And then the beauty of the river scene,
· And ocean in magnificent expanse—
The broad sails moving o'er the wide serene,
　Beneath the sunbeams' variable glance—
The forms which floated on th' unbroken wave—
　The sea-bird, as it cowered in pursuit—
　The vessels passing, not without salute—
The blithe and brief reply their happy sailors gave.

And Isabel—the darling and delight
　Of many fosterers in early day;
·Then, in the bloom of promises more bright,
　Flower of the fair, and loveliest of the gay—
A playful, tender, and ingenuous child,
　Pleased in the partial eyes which welcomed her—
　A maiden joyous, gentle, and sincere,
Who won without essay, and innocently smiled:

When in her glad simplicity she shone
  With modest fascination, undesigned,
And wore a grace surpassing beauty's own,
  That influence revealed her inmost mind.
The springs of Medway, welling from their source,
  Were not more pure, and soft, and bright, than she;
  And when their stream paid tribute to the sea,[12]
It had reflected none so fair in all its course.

Loveliest she was, and brightest, on the morn
  That harbingered affliction in its wane;
Her sweetest hope had silently been worn,
  And unrevealed was her severest pain.
Her joyous spirit chastened and refined,
  The same sincere and gentle heart she bore
  In all her beauty to the convent door,
And left without a look the vacant world behind.

At even she had gained the vessel's prow,
  With her beloved sister hand in hand,
And far beyond her solitary vow
  Felt her reviving, grateful heart expand,
And breathed a name, long registered above,
  But by her lips unuttered; in her heart
  If haply cherished, hid with pious art,
Since its last worldly sigh resigned her maiden love.

When from the field of Bosworth, at her gate,
  Silently sorrowing, Sir Bertram stood—
Partaker of the fortune, not the fate,
  Of him who sealed his duty with his blood,
And had remitted by his last behest
  Her pledge, with lifelong adoration worn,
  And from his clay-cold quivering kisses torn
The latest earthly thing his living lip had pressed—

Permitting then that long-unwonted name—
 "Henry," she said, "devoted, tender friend!
This hope and joy—the dearest I can frame—
 Will soothe my separation to its end.
I see the blessing of a breath divine
 Upon my sister's renovated cheek;
 And seem to hear angelic whispers speak,
Premonishing our souls' reunion—thine and mine."

A smile which earnestly the lady wore
 Refrained in her emotion Isabel:
She paused, and told her pearly chaplet o'er,
 While, downcast with the beads, her eyelids fell.
And yet, this fervent sisterly delight,
 And happy expectation were not all
 That memories of Isabel recall,
Since her exalted soul winged heavenward its flight.

For in the day's severe vicissitude,
 When wind arose to daunt and wave to whelm
The pilot, on his native shore subdued—
 When his tossed bark had answered not her helm,
And quailed the strong beneath the lady's hand,
 Who, while on danger and distress she gazed,
 Extended not the crucifix it raised,
Nor reassurance gave by blessing or command;

Then, Isabel, continually serene
 In virtuous resolve and heavenly peace,
Arose the doubtful and their shrift between,
 As if to bid the wind and waters cease.
And, "Oh, my brothers, penitent and bold,
 May we be sainted in this sign," she said,
 "Whene'er our peril passes human aid,
If such the will above; that time is not yet told."

She said—and many a gallant spirit stirred,
    And swart cheek burned beneath her steadfast eye;
While, with the howling of the storm, were heard
    Reproof and counsel, cheering and reply.
They left the vessel to her fate no more,
    But spread their sail, and, veering with the wind,
    Receded for the anchorage behind,
And set their hope of life upon Reculver's shore.

And did that friendly shore receive them all—
    All, and their poor ungovernable bark?
She weathered well the fury of the squall,
   ` Between the seas and sky, till all was dark—
Then doubled, and recoiled with sudden force;
    And, to a sullenly repeated sound,
    The pilot's with'ring answer was, " We ground! [13]
O miserable men! we strike upon the Horse!"

The seamen sped amain to low'r the boat,
    Amid confusion, terror, cry, and prayer;
But, at the moment when it fell afloat,
    And they had placed the trembling lady there,
And Isabel was almost on its verge—
    The many, to their peril multiplied,
    Who filled it from the ship on ev'ry side,
Were fain to cut adrift, and parted in the surge.

A crew forlorn, on fearful enterprise,
    Amid the tempest, in a bark so frail,
A thousand shapes of death before their eyes,
    One subterfuge alone, and that might fail!
And what had those upon the vessel left?
    Illusions of deliv'rance more remote,
    And doubtful as their parted fellows' lot;
Of ev'ry other hope, except in Heaven, bereft.

Locked lay the vessel, and the water gained
  And broke upon her hull at each rude blast;
And little else for Isabel remained
  Than pious ministrations, ere her last,
To soothe the struggles of th' irreconciled—
  To wean from human loves and charities—
  All that a man may covet as he dies.
And was her sister safe? She augured thus and smiled.

The sun arose upon the water-world
  With gentle airs, and it was all serene;
And every wave as softly, lightly curled,
  As if that yester storm had never been.[14]
And, still unbroken, in its bed of sand
  The bulk of that disordered vessel lay:
  The shoremen saw it as they plied their way,
And bade with lighter hearts a broader sail expand.

Yet there was dew upon the hardy brow,
  Many a cheek flushed, and lifeblood beating fast,
When, now within the vessel's hail, and now
  Impeded by her tackle floating past,
They were aware of none upon her deck.
  But what responses ever rang so dear
  As those which smote upon th' impatient ear
Which first received acclaim of voices from the wreck?

All had survived. They sprang to succour each:
  They bent o'er Isabel's exhausted frame.
She gazed, and struggled eagerly for speech,
  But found her happiest tidings ere it came—
" The lady lives." Her eye inquired no more.
  Feebly she folded hands, and to her breast
  The rescued golden reliquary pressed,
Then gave herself to those who wafted her ashore.

But cold, and wet, and accidents of wreck,
   Were in her image fearfully betrayed,
And somewhat agonizing rose to check
   The welcome which the lady would have bade.
Upon the margin of Reculver's sand
   The first she sprang, and uttered " Isabel ! "
   Then looked into that altered face, and fell,
Relinquishing the hand which touched her sister hand.

Love most affectionate, and gentlest care
   Hovered o'er Isabel, and smoothed her bed ;
But, when the leech had worn the morrow there,
   He spoke despondingly, and hung his head.
Alas, the Lady of St. Clair ! She cried,
   " Me, me, sad authoress of this alone ! [15]
   Improvident, and reckless of mine own,
I left her to the waters ! " Isabel replied—

" Let not your heart be sorrowful in vain ;
   It is the will above, to which I bend.
Heav'n gave one natal hour between us twain,
   And keeps us undivided to the end.
I die in peace, as I have lived ; how blest
   In your dear love, my parting spirit knows.
   Repeat your orisons for its repose,
And leave me where your own remains will sometime rest."

She paused, and colour came into her cheek
   Without a word, and so it passed away ;
And placid, pure, and radiantly meek,
   As if in her beatitude she lay.
The sacrifice of the supremest rite,
   With all its holy prevalence, was paid ;
   Her flutt'ring breath in pious whispers strayed
Upon the crucifix : and this was her good night.

Let others, eloquent in mournful strains,
   Relate the sorrow which the lady bore—
The pomp that waited on those dear remains,
   From sad Reculver brought to Medway's shore,
With psalm, and springlings pure, and holy sign :
   How maidens strewed the freshly flow'ring May,[16]
   And wept, and hung around the beauteous clay,
Exposed in solemn state before her Patron's shrine :

That, when meek sadness came of fond complaint,
   And time went by with healing on his wings,
The relic-casket, vowed to Bradstowe's saint,
   Enriched her treasury of sacred things :
That, for a sister's everlasting rest,
   High mass, with hymns of peace and orisons,
   Was duly chanted by her holiest sons,
And Isabel St. Clair accounted with the blest :

And, that Reculver's church has two fair tow'rs,
   Surnamed from hence "the Sisters of St. Clair" :
The doubtful pilot, as the tempest low'rs,
   May mark their double beacon, and beware.
And here, while saint was sought or requiem sung,
   Upon the morning of the month recurred [17]
   Continual Litany, no longer heard
Those wild-careering waves and hollow sands among.

They leave for me—how, all devoutly willed
   By Isabel in her supreme request,
The lady's piety and fate fulfilled,
   Their earthly relics reunited rest
Beneath a spot on Medway's brink, unseen;
   But, while St. Benedict had household stone,
   Or sanctuary to his servants known,
There was none holier place without his silver screen.

There, hand in hand, their images had kneeled
    Before a cross, in Benedictine stole;
A saintly legend at their feet revealed
    What has survived beyond the brazen scroll,
And may be meet for simple bard to tell—
    The memory of that endearing name
    Which, in their pilgrimage, so well became
The Lady of St. Clair, and Sister Isabel.

NOTES.

INTRODUCTION.

[1] *My guide awaits me.*

This Poem was occasioned by a visit, in 1822, to the venerable church of Reculver, in the Isle of Thanet; as described in the Introduction. The incidents of the story are supplied from "Keate's Sketches," a transcript of the text of which is subjoined. History is silent as to the truth of them, but the narrative accords with the traditions of the county. It may be remarked, however, that there is no account of any monastic institution for females at Faversham or in the neighbourhood, except Davington Priory, the remains of which, still existing, do not claim the splendour and consequence attributed in the narrative to the house over which Frances St. Clair is therein stated to have presided.

[2] *Sacred too soon to the departed guest.*

Dr. Pemberton, who died at Fredville, Kent, the house of his brother-in-law, July 24th, 1822.

[3] *As in Samaria by the prophet laid to rest.*

"And the prophet took up the carcass of the man of God, and laid it upon the ass, and brought it back; and the old prophet came to the city to mourn, and to bury him.

"And he laid his carcass in his own grave; and they mourned over him, saying, 'Alas, my brother!'"

1 KINGS, chap. 13.

[4] *A pass untried,*
And lightly buoyant on the trembling tide.

Grove Ferry.

[5] *A vestige that Severus' castle stood,*
The royal house of Ethelbert; the bower
By Eadred given to be a saintly dower.

"It is said, Severus, Emperor of Rome, about the year 205 built a castle at this place, which he fortified against the Britons;

that Ethelbert, one of the Kings of Kent, erected a palace here for himself and his successors; and that, about two hundred years after, a monastery was erected here, which, in the year 949, King Eadred gave with the manor to Christchurch, Canterbury. The dredgers for oysters on this coast, which are reckoned exceedingly good, have often met in the sands with Roman vessels, cisterns, cellars, &c., besides vast numbers of Roman coins, rings, and bracelets, which came from the land by the fall of the cliffs.

"The sea has got so much of this town, that there are but few houses left; and its church was in such danger, above twenty years ago, that men were almost continually employed to make good the walls or banks."

ENGLAND'S GAZETTEER, 1751.

6 *Yet has Reculver's venerable fane*
Its station on the relics of the land.

"The west door is a pointed arch of Caen stone, with Saxon ornaments, much decayed. There is a pediment at the west end, between the two spires.

"The floor was laid in terras, made of coarse stone and mortar, so smooth as to seem polished, being thinly encrusted with a red composition."

"In this church the body of King Ethelbert is said to have been buried. And Weever says, in his time (that is, King James the First's reign) there was remaining at the upper end of the south aisle a monument of an antique form, mounted with two spires, beneath which, according to tradition, this monarch lay; but no remains of the monument are left."

HASTED, HIST. KENT.

"The remains of the church of Reculver are now the property of the Corporation of the Trinity House. The forms of spires are preserved by framework on the top of each of the Sister Towers, for the purpose of a seamark.

PART I.

7 *Within that chapel of the Virgin loved*
And graced by miracles and cures divine.

"A chapel consecrated to the Virgin, at Broadstowe, or Broadstairs, in the Isle of Thanet, and in which her image was esteemed to work such great miracles that pilgrims came from parts very remote to visit it; and it was held in such veneration, that all ships passing within sight of it are reported constantly to have lowered their topsails to salute it."

C 2

[8] *In honour of th' Invention of the Cross.*

The festival of the Invention of the Cross is on the third day of May, as noted in our calendar. The voyage of the sisters, for the pùrpose of being present at the celebration of the festival at Bradstow, is recorded to have begun on the first of the month.

[9] *All in their solemn weeds of wool undyed,*
And sable stole, and hood, and scapular.

"St. Benedict, a native of Nursia, in the dukedom of Spoleto, in Italy, was born about the year 480, and died about the year 543. His rule was not confirmed until fifty-two years after his death, when it received the sanction of Pope Gregory the Great.

"There were nuns of this order, as well as monks. Their habit was a black robe, with a scapulary of the same, under which was a tunic of undyed wool; and when they went to the choir, they had, over all, a black cowl, like that worn by the monks."

GROSE, ANTIQ., Preface.

[10] *Which met the tide where Thames and Swale unite.*

"Sheppy Island is encompassed by the East and West Swale, two branches of the Medway, which here fall into the Thames."

ENGLAND'S GAZETTEER.

[11] *Lo, lady! we were lost, and have been found*
Through him who laboured thus a night and day.

"Thrice have I suffered shipwreck; a night and a day have I been in the deep."

ST. PAUL, 2 Cor., chap. 11.

PART II.

[12] *And when their stream paid tribute to the sea,*
It had reflected none so fair in all its course.

"Phœbus, on fleetest coursers borne,
Sees none so fair in all his race."

OLD SONG.

[13] *We ground!*
O miserable men! we strike upon the Horse.

"A bank of sand, called the 'Horse,' which lies a little off from Reculver."

KEATE.

[14] *As if that yester storm had never been.*

"—— remoter from the scene,
Where, but for him, that strife had never been,
A breathing but devoted warrior lay."

LARA, Canto 2.

[15] *Me, me, sad authoress of this alone.*

" Me, me, adsum qui feci."

NISUS.—Virg. Æn. ix. 427.

[16] *How maidens strewed the freshly flow'ring May.*

The white thorn is often noticed by writers of monastic legends as symbolical of purity and saintship.

[17] *Upon the morning of the month recurred
Continual Litany.*

Instituted by the Lady of St. Clair; the shipwreck fatal to her sister having taken place on the first day of the month.

FROM "KEATE'S SKETCHES."

SEVERAL years ago, being on a journey to Spa, I was detained some time in the University of Louvain by an accidental illness, which seized me on the road. During my stay I made an acquaintance with an Irish Jesuit, who honoured me with many civilities, and whom I found a very intelligent companion. He showed me whatever he thought most curious in the place; though, except the great library and the public schools, there is but little worth notice.

I was, however, much pleased with two manuscript volumes which I met with in the library of one of the colleges. They chiefly contained anecdotes relative to some English families, and to several historical and monastical antiquities, and were the memorials of a Dominican Friar of Canterbury, who quitted England at the time of the Reformation, and retired to Louvain. At his death he bequeathed them, with other curious books, to the College where they were. My friend, who was one of its members, procured the manuscript for me; and in turning over many subjects far less interesting, I met with the historical account of this church (Reculver). I have divested it of the obsolete language of the times, but the substance of it is nearly as follows :—

Towards the end of those troublesome times, when England was shaken by the feuds of the Houses of York and Lancaster, there resided in a village on the banks of the Medway a gentleman whose name was Geoffry de St. Clair, descended from a family of great antiquity and repute in those parts. The many lances and pieces of armour which hung around the old hall did not render it more respectable than did the unbounded benevolence of its possessor. The poor sat at his gate and blessed his liberal hand; and never a pilgrim reposed in his porch without remembering in his orisons its hospitable owner.

St. Clair had allied himself in marriage with the Lady Margaret de Boys, a woman of high birth and rare endowments; whose accomplishments might have embellished the greatest scenes, had not a love of domestic life and a religious cast of mind induced her to prefer retirement. All her leisure hours which her family did not call for were spent in duties which, in that age, ladies of the noblest rank exercised, without thinking that they demeaned their stations. She relieved the indigent, advised with the unfortunate, visited the sick, and brought up her twin daughters, Frances and Isabella, in the same sentiments, accustoming them very early to attend her in all these acts of primitive piety.

As these young ladies were the sole issue of St. Clair and Lady Margaret, they devoted their whole attention to their education; and had the comfort to find in their minds so rich a soil, that everything prospered which was planted in it. No useful knowledge was omitted, no external accomplishment neglected.

Frances and Isabella were now arrived at the age of twenty-five. The amiableness of their characters, their enlarged understandings, and the gracefulness of their persons, won the admiration and esteem of all who approached them. They had, from similitude of manners and sentiment, contracted so rare an affection for each other, that it seemed as if Nature, by forming them together in the womb, had prepared them for that extraordinary union which was to distinguish their lives, and for those effusions of elevated friendship which the loss of their exemplary mother was one day to call forth. Nor was this event very remote. Lady Margaret was seized by a sudden illness, which in a few days carried her off, and desolated one of the happiest families in the world.

It would be difficult to describe the sounds of woe which on this occasion echoed through all the mansion, or the sighs of the disconsolate poor under the windows. The grief of St. Clair, after the many years of uninterrupted happiness that he had enjoyed with Lady Margaret, in its first attack almost overpowered his reason; whilst Frances and Isabella had the weight of a father's sorrow added to their own, which compelled them to smother their feelings, and to assume a fortitude which their hearts disavowed. Though St. Clair called in all his philosophy to support himself under the loss of his beloved Lady Margaret, yet he was worn by a silent sorrow, which had so visible an effect on his health as to endanger his life, and which in about a year put an end to it.

In this mournful interval, the greatest comfort his dejected daughters received was from the frequent visits of their uncle, John de St. Clair, who was at that time Abbot of the Monastery of St. Augustin, in Canterbury, of which place there are at this day such noble remains existing. He was the younger brother of Geoffry, though there was but the difference of a year between them; and was reputed to be a man of so much learning and virtue, that St. Clair, by his will, recommended his children to his care and protection, bequeathing to each of them a very large inheritance.

The manner in which Frances had been brought up, added to her natural turn of mind and the example of a mother whom she so much revered, determined her to a life of religious retirement; and a great convent of Benedictine nuns, not very distant from Faversham, happening a few months after to lose their Principal (who was always one of a considerable family), the Abbot of St. Augustin, perceiving her fixed in her scheme of life, procured her to be named the Lady Abbess of it.

Isabella, who had never as yet been separated from her sister, would on this occasion most willingly have taken the veil. "The same roof," says she, "hath ever, hitherto, covered us—the same have been our wishes, the same our pursuits. The grave hath divided us from those who taught us the amiableness of friendship, and shall alone divide us from one another."

The Abbot was much hurt by this declaration of his niece. He desired her to banish from her thoughts such a resolution; and failed not to intimate to her that, Frances having devoted herself to the cloister, she remained the only support of the family of St. Clair— that her virtues should rather embellish society than be lost within the walls of a monastery; and wished she would, by accepting some alliance of suitable rank and fortune, rather permit those accomplishments to be seen by the world which she sought to hide in oblivion.

Frances, on her part, however she was charmed with this testimony of her sister's affection, joined in sentiment with her uncle, expressing to her how much happier she should be to see her settle herself by marriage, and imitate the good life and example of their excellent mother. "I am not, you know,'" she said, "by the religious office I fill, tied down to all those rites which must, of course, be imposed upon you; my liberty remains. We shall have constant opportunities of continuing that intercourse of love our hearts so mutually desire. It will be the highest pleasure to me to see you united to a man worthy your choice, preserving in our father's castle that hospitality for which it hath so long been famed; and whenever you wish to make a short retreat from the bustle of the world, our holy house will afford you a peaceable asylum."

It was not without great difficulty, nor even till much time after, that, by the repeated solicitations of Frances and her uncle, Isabella was prevailed on to relinquish entirely her intentions of entering into a monastic life. She resided for some time in her father's venerable old mansion on the Medway, accompanied by a widowed aunt, her father's sister, who at intervals attended her on visits to Frances, and also, at particular seasons, to the Abbot, at his house, which was a noble building adjoining to the monastery of St. Augustin.

It was in one of these visits to the Abbot that she became acquainted with Henry de Belville, between whose father and the Abbot there had long subsisted a most firm friendship. He was of good birth, though much inferior to Isabella in fortune, his father's estate having greatly suffered in the confusion of those turbulent times.

Belville was now in his twenty-ninth year. His figure was graceful and manly; and to a disposition as amiable as his person was joined an understanding both quick and strong, which had been improved by the most extensive education that the fashion of the age allowed. He had been sent to travel over Europe, had resided in several of its principal courts, and was now on his return from a short expedition into France, and had stopped at Canterbury to pay his respects to the Abbot, and to deliver him certain letters with which he had been charged.

Belville, on his first return to England, a few years previous to the present period, had been honoured by the patronage of Richard, Duke of Gloucester, near whose person he held an employment which could not long dispense with his absence; for that prince being now mounted on the throne of England, the whole kingdom was thrown into a hostile state.

It will not be wondered at, if, after Belville and Isabella had been a few days together, their mutual accomplishments, and their mutual desire to please, should have made them much charmed with one another. Belville felt himself enamoured of his fair companion, and had the satisfaction to perceive that his attention to her was not thrown away. Though he took leave, after a short time, to go to London, yet he found an excuse for returning very soon; and having reason to think he had made a favourable impression on Isabella, did not long hesitate to propose himself to her as one who would be happy to pass his life in the society of so engaging a woman. His offer was not less pleasing to Isabella than it was to her uncle and Frances, the latter of whom proposed to give up to her sister her right in the castle of St. Clair, where it was intended they should reside.

Everything was preparing for their nuptials, and nothing could wear a fairer face of prosperity than did this proposed union of true and disinterested affection; but the successful progress that the arms of Henry of Richmond now made in the kingdom had obliged Richard to oppose them with his utmost force, and to summon all his servants to attend his camp—among whom, as I before mentioned, was the intended bridegroom, who at this time would most willingly have waived the service, had not his own nice sense of honour, and his zeal for his royal master, overcome every private consideration.

Were I to follow closely the manuscript from which the substance of this story is drawn, it would lead me into some of the historical transactions of those times, which are already sufficiently known: only it is worthy of being remembered, that there are encomiums bestowed on the character and person of Richard, upon both of which historians have thrown so much deformity. I shall therefore pass over these circumstances, which are foreign to my subject, and only observe that the unfortunate Belville was among those of the King's followers who shared the fate of their royal master in Bosworth field. He was near Richard in a great part of the battle, and was also a witness of his death; and, his own horse being killed under him, either by the fall, or by being trampled on in the confusion, his thigh was broken; and after Richmond's party had obtained the victory, this gallant youth was carried, with several others, wounded, into Leicester, where, his rank being known, he was lodged in a monastery of Black Friars in that city. His page, Bertram, who had served him from his infancy, took care that every assistance should be procured for him; but the fever which was occasioned by the accident, together with the many bruises he had received, neither gave himself nor those about him any other prospect than that of his approaching death.

Those who contemplate Belville a few weeks before, in the full vigour of youth, flattering himself with every expectation of happiness which virtue, fortune, and a union with one of the loveliest of women could present to his imagination, and now picture him stretched on a poor pallet, surrounded by a parcel of mendicant friars, his countenance shrunk and wan, and his eyes fixed with humility and resignation on a crucifix which they held before him, cannot, surely, by the contrast, avoid dropping a sigh at the fallacy of human hopes.

A little while before he expired, he desired to be left alone with his page, that he might give him his latest orders. "Bertram," he said, looking wistfully at him, "the day which hath ruined our sovereign's fortune, hath blasted mine; and that, too, in the moment when it shone the fairest. Thou wilt soon render me the last of thy faithful services. Let my body rest with the fathers of this house, and, as soon as thou hast seen its due rites performed, speed thee to Canterbury, and acquaint the holy Abbot of St. Augustin with the bloody event of yesterday; conjure him that he unfold it to my intended bride in such manner as his discretion shall advise. Bear her this jewel from my finger, in token that my last thoughts dwelt on her; and tell her my only sigh, in leaving the world, was for losing her, whose virtues so embellished it."

The faithful Bertram dropped a tear of affection and gratitude over the grave of his gallant master, and, journeying to Canterbury with a bursting heart, presented himself before the Abbot with such a countenance as scarcely needed a tongue to tell his melancholy errand.

The arrival of Belville's page could not long be a secret to Isabella, who was then at her uncle's, and whose mind instantly foreboded some extraordinary event; though the news of the battle had not yet reached that city.

When St. Clair found himself sufficiently composed to open the mournful business to his niece, he spared none of that ghostly comfort which a good man would offer on such an occasion; though the amount of all that can be said to the sons and daughters of affliction is no more than this, that it is our duty and our interest to bear with patience that which it is not in our power to alter. The exertions of nature must subside before the soothing voice of reason can be heard.

Isabella, after giving way to the first transports of passion, assumed a fortitude and resignation which her piety alone could inspire. She desired that Bertram might be detained two or three days at the monastery, and, as soon as her mind was more fortified, she would despatch him to her sister Frances, whom she could then bear to see with more calmness, and to whom she sent a letter by the hands of the page.

When the Lady Abbess saw her sister, she found her confirmed in a resolution of entering on a monastic life; her uncle, conceiving it might best restore a calm to her troubled spirits, no longer opposed it; and, as soon as her affairs were properly adjusted and everything prepared, she took the veil in the convent where Frances presided.

Isabella found in religion the only consolation for her past misfortunes; and although the remembrance of her beloved Belville would often come across her, and spread a temporary gloom over her mind, yet she constantly strove to dispel it by piety and resignation. The two sisters enjoyed all that heartfelt pleasure which arises from rooted friendship; and, as the effect of benevolent dispositions operates on all around, theirs served to communicate happiness to all the sisterhood.

The Louvain manuscript informs us that, after these ladies had passed nearly fourteen years in this peaceful retirement, the Abbess was seized with an alarming fever, the effects of which hung so long upon her that they greatly endangered her life. It is not difficult to conceive how severe Isabella's sufferings were in this interval of suspense and apprehension, or the anxieties of her mind until her sister was restored to health.

Frances, during her illness, had made a private vow to the blessed Virgin Mary that, if she recovered, she would send some costly offering to a chapel which was consecrated to her, at a little port called Bradstowe, or Broadstairs, in the Isle of Thanet (part of which chapel is at this day remaining), and in which her image was esteemed to work such great miracles that pilgrims came from parts very remote to visit it; and it was held in such veneration, that all ships, passing within sight of it, are reported constantly to have lowered their topsails to salute it. And the feast of the Invention of the Holy Cross, which was the third day of May, being to be celebrated there with great solemnity, her gratitude for her recovery and for the supposed intercession of the Virgin determined her to go herself at that time, and fulfil her vow.

Isabella obtained permission to accompany her sister on this devout purpose; and, the roads being little frequented in that age, and a horse almost the only conveyance, they resolved to put themselves, with two attendants, aboard a passage sloop that usually went at stated times from Faversham to Broadstairs, and other parts along the coast between that place and the Downs.

They set sail in the evening; but had not been at sea above two hours, before a violent storm arose. Everyone who is acquainted with the navigation of this coast, quite to the mouth of the Thames, knows how difficult it is rendered by reason of the many flats and banks of sand that obstruct it.

The suddenness and fury of the storm, together with the thunder and lightning which accompanied it, threw a dismay among all the passengers; and the mariners, from the opposition of the wind and tide, were unable to direct the vessel—to pursue their course was impracticable. They therefore attempted to save themselves by running in on the shore, at a place called Reculver (which is a small village, though of great antiquity, situate on the borders of the Isle of Thanet); but the advance of night and a thick fog prevented them from discerning exactly whereabouts they were. Every endeavour to reach the shore was frustrated by the storm driving them from it; and their sails being all shattered, a sudden swell of the sea bore them quite out of their direction, and struck the vessel on a bank of sand called the " Horse," that lies a little off Reculver.

The surprise, the confusion, and the image of death that must naturally rush into the minds of people who are on the point of being wrecked, can only be justly felt or described by those who have stood in so dreadful a situation. Each one recommended himself to God and to his tutelar saint. The mariners hoisted out their longboat as precipitately as they could; and that which most agitated the thoughts of Frances and Isabella was the mutual preservation of each other.

Scarce was the boat upon the surface of the waves, when everyone was eager to rush into it; for it was certain the vessel must bulge in a few hours, and, to add to the horror, night advanced.

The captain, almost by force, dragged the Lady Abbess and her sister from the cabin; and scarce had he helped the first, half dead as she was, down the side of the ship, when those who were already in the boat, finding they must all perish if more got in, pushed off instantly and rowed towards shore, in spite of the menaces of the

captain, who stood on deck supporting Isabella, the entreaties of
the Abbess, who was wild to return, and the cries of the passengers
left behind.

The only faint hope which now remained to those on board was
that the vessel might possibly hold together till some assistance
could be obtained from the shore, which they still flattered them-
selves would come, in case the boat reached the land, which pro-
videntially it did, though with the utmost risk. Everyone who
remained in the vessel was resigned to his fate; and, surrounded as
Isabella was by impending death, it afforded no small consolation to
her to think there was a possibility that her sister had escaped.

It was four hours after the arrival of the boat before anyone
durst venture out; when, the storm abating with the departure of
the tide, and the day being near dawning, a large boat put off to the
wreck. When those who went to assist got to it, they found all the
people on board retired to different places beneath the deck, great
part of which was broken away. Isabella had remained in the
cabin, one side of which was also washed away, and the room half
filled with water. She was almost exhausted by the terrors she
had sustained, the bruises she had received, and the extreme cold in
which she had so long suffered. They led her with the utmost
gentleness from this wretched place, while she, all pale and trem-
bling, scarcely comprehended at first what they were doing; yet
life seemed to flush anew in her countenance on hearing that her
sister was preserved.

As soon as they had brought her on shore, she was supported by
several women, who were waiting to receive her, and conducted her
to the house were the Lady Abbess was. Frances, transported
at the first sight of her sister, ran out to meet Isabella, who, at the
moment she approached, made an effort to spring forward to her,
but sunk down overpowered in the arms of her attendants. Frances
clasped her hand, and, in her eager joy, would have uttered some-
thing, but could only faintly pronounce her name, and fell at her feet
in a swoon.

Isabella was immediately put into bed, and received every as-
sistance that could be procured; but her strength and spirits were so
exhausted by the terror and fatigue which her mind and body had
undergone, and by remaining so many hours in water, that she
lived but till the evening of the following day.

Frances, though still sinking from the shock and agitation of the preceding night, forgot, in her attention to her sister, her own sufferings. She never stirred from her bedside, and often accused herself as being the fatal cause of all that had befallen her, by suffering her attendance on this expedition. Isabella chid her for thinking so, declaring it was the will of Heaven, to which she patiently submitted. "Though we came into the world together," she said, "yet, as we were not destined to perish together, a time must inevitably have come when death would have dissolved our union. I rejoice that I am not the survivor; I die, where I have ever wished to live, in the arms of the most beloved of sisters. Pray for the repose of my soul, and lay me in the tomb which you have allotted to be your own, that one grave may in death hold our remains who, in life, had but one heart."

The loss of Isabella plunged the Lady Abbess into that deep distress which minds formed, like hers, with the noblest sentiments of tenderness and benevolence, must on such a trial inevitably feel. She caused the body of her unfortunate sister to be transported in solemnity to their convent, where, after it had been exposed with accustomed rites, it was deposited, with every mark of respect, in a vault on one side the shrine of St. Benedict, bedewed with tears of the most heartfelt sorrow, dropped from the eyes of all the sisterhood..

When time and reflection had somewhat calmed her affliction, Frances failed not to transmit by the hands of her confessor (her uncle the Abbot having been some time dead) her intended offering to the Virgin of Broadstairs, accompanied by a donation of twelve masses to be said for the repose of Isabella's soul; and soon after, to perpetuate the memory of her sister, as well as to direct mariners in their course, that they might escape the sad calamity herself had so fatally experienced, she caused a very ancient church, which stood on a rising ground just above the village of Reculver, and which was greatly fallen into decay, to be restored and much enlarged; and at one end thereof she erected two towers, with lofty spires upon them, which she directed should be called "the Sisters," and to this day they retain the name, and are a seamark of great utility.

In less than seven years the whole church was completed, which she endowed very liberally, by a grant out of her own fortune, and

ordained that there should be celebrated one solemn mass on the
first day of every month (the wreck having happened on the first
day of May), and that a perpetual Litany should be sung for the
eternal peace of the departed Isabella. She lived to see this her
will executed, as well as to bestow many other charitable donations,
not only on the convent over which she presided, but on several
other religious institutions; and was, from her amiable character
and pious example, beloved and respected to the last hour of her
life.

She survived Isabella eleven years, and died, most sincerely and
deservedly lamented, towards the end of the year 1512. Her re-
mains, pursuant to her own desire, were deposited by the side of those
of her sister, with all that solemnity due to her high rank and office.
A monument was erected near to the place where they were interred,
with their figures kneeling hand in hand before a cross, and,
beneath it, a plate of brass, recording their unshaken friendship.

Mina.

FROM MEDWIN'S "CONVERSATIONS OF LORD BYRON."

"THERE were two stories, which he (Lewis) almost believed by telling. One happened to himself, whilst he was residing at Manheim;" "the other was the original of his 'Alonzo and Imogine,'[1] which has had such a host of imitators. Two Florentine lovers, who had been attached to each other almost from childhood, made a vow of eternal fidelity. Mina was the name of the lady; her husband's I forget, but it is not material. They parted. He had been for some time absent with his regiment, when, as his disconsolate lady was sitting alone in her chamber, she distinctly heard the well known sound of his footsteps, and, starting up, beheld—not her husband, but his spectre, with a deep ghastly wound across his forehead, entering. She swooned with horror. When she recovered, the ghost told her that, in future, his visits should be announced by a passing bell, and these words distinctly whispered: 'Mina, I am here!'

"Their interviews now became frequent, till the woman fancied herself as much in love with the ghost as she had been with the man. But it was soon to prove otherwise. One fatal night she went to a ball. What business had she there? She danced, too; and, what was worse, her partner was a young Florentine, so much the counterpart of her lover, that she became estranged from his ghost. Whilst the young gallant conducted her in the waltz, and her ear drank in the music of his voice and words, a passing bell tolled! She had been accustomed to the sound till it hardly excited her attention; and now, lost in the attractions of her fascinating partner, she heard but regarded it not. A second peal! she listened not to its warnings. A third time the bell, with its deep and iron tongue, startled the assembled company, and silenced the music! Mina then turned her eyes from her partner, and saw reflected in the mirror a form, a shadow, a spectre: it was her husband! He was standing between her and the young Florentine, and whispered, in a solemn and melancholy tone, the accustomed - accents—'Mina, I am here!' She instantly fell dead."

PART I.

Is there a love so pure
 And so affectionate,
It ever shall endure,
 Above the tyranny of fate,
In all vicissitudes of things,
When youth and joy have flown on halcyon wings—
 When life has but satieties,
 When its extremest sparkle dies—
 And then, renewed,
A little lovelier than before,
But nothing more,
 Unless for the beatitude,
Shall bear its sparkle in the sky,
Unchanged, unchangeably?
And to such spirit be resigned,
 By guardians above,
Their ministration in the mind
 Of its divided love—
To draw from each idea stain
Of aught ungenerous or vain;
To guard the thoughts, as they arise
 In aspiration from the breast,
 Serenest, humblest, loveliest—
A mental offering, unseen by mortal eyes;
 And only yield to higher care
 When grief or ill would mingle there?

Th' adopted spirit, too, may feel
   Communion deep and strange;
Acceptance it may not reveal,
   Would not for worlds exchange?
     Such, chronicles record,
Florentine Mina felt of her Etrurian lord.

Their life began, their young affection grew,
   Where Arno wanders in his native plains—[2]
     The beautiful domains
Of blushing grape, and flow'r-bloom ever new,
     Beneath the mighty line
     Of the protecting Apennine,
And Fiesole, the cypress-tufted hill,
   Mid of the mountain and the brow
   Apparelled in perennial snow,
Whence constant streams distil.
In infancy they lingered, hand in hand,
Upon the margin of that lovely strand,
   Inhaling sweets as they arose.
Their after friendship, which refined
The first impressions of the mind,
   Was artlessness, and unrestrained as those.

The boast of Tuscan chivalry their line,
   Equal to both in fortune and in fame;
And parents looked with augury benign
   Upon the rising of the mutual flame.
Then grew the sprightly graceful hour
Of youth's emprise and beauty's power;
 And, dearer still, the circle round
 Each sweetly conscious bosom wound,
"And, if the holy Virgin e'er received
   A faithful lover's oath"
(So vowed the youth, the maiden so believed,
   And plighted troth for troth)—

" The heart I pledge to thee
    Shall never, never more be free;
The love, indissolubly one
    In life, be prevalent in death,
Be of our earthliness alone
    Resigned not with the breath!
If Heav'n divide our fatal hour,
    The mystic bond shall be the same,
        A sacrament to bind
        The pilgrim and the parted mind;
Shall be alone the blissful dower,
    The reunited claim!
        Our Lady so decree,
        As I have vowed to thee."

And many a vesper sank upon the blush
    Of Mina, joyful in her mystic vow;
While, radiant with love and hope, the flush
    Beamed on her coronal-encircled brow;
And tender passion, faithfully returned,
In such simplicity and calmness burned,
    It seemed that earth had not beside,
Nor paradise, a dearer claim
Than they had imaged in the name
    Of husband and of bride.
Whether, the brightest of the gay, they trode
    In full saloon and colonnade;
Or paused, admiring, in the rare abode,
The temple, of the Ausonian Muse,[3]
    Where taste and genius had arrayed
        The mimic form divine
        In all the magic of th' evolving line,
And harmony of hues—
Whether they joined the votive throng
Those dim arcades and domes among,

Where sleep the Medicean race,[4]
Each in his gorgeous restingplace;
But one sepulchral stone
Is rich in Cosmo's name alone—
Whether they wandered on that hill, the same
Whence Buonaroti drew the immortal flame,[5]
Or Galileo read the skies [6]
     By art before unknown,
Or Dante pondered mysteries[7]
     Perchance to be their own—
Still, still, fidelity supreme
     In its unchanging power,
Ruled, as its votaries might deem,
     An ever circling hour.
'Twas only at some interval,
When troubled fancy might recall
     The solemn and peculiar doom
         Invited by their vow,
     That an involuntary gloom
         Impressed each youthful brow.

By trumpet call and clash of steel,
     Ausonia marshalled her array;
'Twas freedom's brave appeal.
     Then, who would indolently stray,
         And watch the noontide beams
         Beside her sunny streams?
A gath'ring voice which filled the air,
The foot of multitudes, was there;
         There, ever and anon revealed,
     Some banderol, which shook and fell
         Above the bristling field;
     Or wave of plumy swell,
Or leader's crest, and falchion bright,
Emerging into light;

Or form which urged to speed
The still curvetting steed.
Vanward of all that glorious war,
  A youthful hero moved;
And yet his looks were wandering far,
  Averted from the field he loved,
     And anxiously set
    Upon the distant parapet,
And one unconscious form reclined
  Beneath its embrasure;
A moment since, he left behind
  That heart most fond and pure—
    How will they meet again?
Shudd'ring, as if in mortal pain,
He murmured, " Mina," and was lost
    Among the marching host.
     And every morn and eve
    Mina beheld the place
Where she had met his last embrace,
  And he had disappeared;
    And lingered long, to grieve,
    And utter there, unheard,
Some faithful vow or pious strain,
Repeated oft and oft again.
  To cast a trembling glance
    Upon the silent vale,
  Or at each image in advance
    To faulter and turn pale,
     Misdoubting of the bold
    Some peril yet untold.

The sun had left the western sky
Beneath a gorgeous canopy
  Of gold and amarant;
And as the glory fell aslant

Upon the battled stone,
Each rugged form which met the sight
Received from the departing light
A strange unreal tone.
By Mina, when she passed the spot,
A shadow seemed to glide.
Twice it approached her, and was not;
Once, ere her timid eyes withdrew,
Appeared to gain a living hue—
Then vanished by her side.
A sense of evil undefined
Oppressed her solitary mind;
And while she tottered from the wall,
With feeble step and slow,
And hardly reached her silent hall,
She thought upon her vow.
She gained her bridal bower, alone
Its melancholy guest.
Dull echoes of a footstep pressed,
Advancing on her own;
They rang within the corridor,
And moved along the marble floor—
They met her ear.
Surprise and joy had baffled fear;
She sprang—a thousand welcomes hung
In rapture on her tongue,
Accusing each its own delay.
Between her and the portal still unclosed
A form had interposed.
She looked, and died away.
Perfect its lineaments; the mien
Such as her wedded lord's had been;
And, moving in the gloom around,
By visionary light—
Object impalpable, it met her sight,
Her ear received its sound.

And though an impress of his lot
  Was written on the ensanguined face,
    And each regard was sad and slow,
Yet still the expression varied not
  From his who left her last embrace,
Affectionate and mild, alas! as even now.

    Poor Mina! when, again,
  The thoughts pursued their sad career
    In her bewildered brain
Deemed yet her spirit-husband near,
  Her bridal chamber and saloon
  Were lighted by the crescent moon.
    Its argentry reposed
On ev'ry flow'r with chalice closed
    Around her balcony;
  So calm and soft the airs abroad
  Were visiting her lute's light chord,
    It slept untremblingly.
" And has fidelity like ours
    For recompense but this?
    Is such our promised bliss?"
She murmured, when the tearful show'rs,
    Descending on her cheek,
    Permitted her to speak.
  A slowly-cadent symphony
  Of requiem music floated by—
A well known speech, solemn and still, was there,
    Responsive in the air.
" Bethink thee, love! the saints allow
    Between us twain
    The yet enduring vow.
  A sacrament doth bind
The pilgrim and the parted mind
    Until we meet again;
  And Mina has to prove,

Through every maze
In which her spirit strays,
The presence of her love."
" Presence ineffably more welcome now
Than ever while my love was' young"
(The faithful accents fell from Mina's tongue)—
" I ratify my vow.
But, oh! the form which met my sight,
Incarnadined, as if from dreadful fight"——
" The form which told my fate shall ne'er
Again appear"
(The spirit's voice replied);
" But, with the dying requiem tone,
This greeting—Mina, I am here!—alone
Proclaim me by thy side."
She stretched her hands in empty space,
As if to find once more that dear embrace;
Then, kneeling, crossed her brow,
And called the saints again to ratify her vow.

PART II.

Alas! should heav'n, attested, not redeem
    The frail and erring from their bond,
  To live were but a mingled dream
    Of fascination and despond—
Of light and darkness to be felt; [8]
    While images illusive flit
      Before the vacant eye,
    And tunes the changing chords emit
      Are dissonance, not harmony,
At which the heart would melt.
Rescue from such were happy; happier yet,
  Ne'er to have linked the visionary chain;
  Happiest, to guide by precept pure and plain
The livelong hours, till nature claim her debt;
    And then, at evening close,
Resign the unburthened spirit to repose
      With humble prayer,
Casting on Heav'n to-morrow's care.

      Yet Mina wore
The widowhood of her peculiar choice
  In meek seclusion, which alike forbore
To welcome or reject a monitory voice:
Such had her gentle ear—her thanks repaid
    The kindly proffered aid;
Her confidence was shared with none:

Some fascination seemed to fall
    Upon each interval
    She passed alone.
The lifting of her sable veil
Disclosed a brow serenely pale—
Fixed eyes, that from the lucid sky
Seemed gathering their brilliancy;
Deeming the while aught earthly nothing less
    Than vanity and selfishness.
The damsel chosen from her train
    To guard her privacy,
Perchance had heard a frequent strain
    Of airy music floating by—
Plaintive and soothing, like the praise
Which pious men, and, haply, angels raise
    Around a form composed
    Upon the bier;
    And, as the requiem closed,
    The listener dropped a tear,
    Which fondly stole
Amid her orisons for some departed soul.

Those hours had waned—the gathered sorrow slept
    With time's relinquished store,
And, radiant in beauty, Mina stepped
    Again on Arno's vernal flow'ry shore;
The gallant and the blithe around,
    Who greeted and resigned the day
    With canzonet or roundelay,
    By viol's sound.
They met the beautiful recluse
    With welcomes such as playmates bring,
Or friends and lovers use
    After long absence hastening;

They led her to the redolent parterre,
　The gondola upon the stream,
　　The circle and the galliard[9]
　　Along the fresh green sward.
Could Mina's heart forbear?
　As if unburthened of a dream,
　　It followed in the sport,
　　Herself the grace of each resort,
And let the busy triflers have
Attention cold but now, and wedded to the grave.
　Not that among the smiles she lent
　　　Immingled aught
　　　Accuser of her lightest thought;
Yet still her colour came and went,
As solemn memory possessed
　　　Her conscious breast;
　　　For, oh! the frolic scene
　Had shed its liveliness between
　　Divided musings many a one,
　Like full blown rosaries,
Casting their fragrance and their dyes
　Around some monumental stone.

Mina had vowed unfeignedly : her heart,
　In that gay clime of pleasure unreproved,
Had spotless held its fealty apart
　　For him she loved.
　　Yet, in the sublunary state,
　　Vicissitude, alas! is fate;
　　　Solicitings arise,
　Present though slight, and claim regard
　For trifles any moment may award,
　　How transient soe'er, while yet realities;
And faithful vows which left a lover's tongue,
And darling hopes to which affection clung,

Losing their object, vainly are enshrined
　　Within the widowed mind.
The joyous season of the Italian year,[10]
　　Grown from its birth to early spring,
Held Florence in her fond career
　　Of mimicry and revelling;
At ev'ry bell proclaiming noon,
　　In their extravagance of guise,
The masquer and buffoon
　　Renewed their quaint solemnities;
Gayest and loudest, when the merry crew
Had days of abstinence in nearer view:
　　Their chariots rolled in double line,
Proceeding and repassing each
　　Amid a shower of haildrops saccharine,
With gallantry and jest in every form and speech.
　　The tapestry, of ample fold,
Descended in its weight of gold
　　From gallery and seat,
And there the loveliness of all the land,
Assuming each her beautiful command,
　　Beheld the crowded street;
Then left its pageantries behind
For hours of pleasure more refined,
When there was music or the party made,
Or gay festino filled the bright arcade.[11]

　　Thither conducted by the joyous train,
Had Mina sometimes stayed, perchance
To note the movement of the dance,
　　Or listen to the strain;
Disclaiming yet the charm that ruled
　　The pleasure-world around—
The trifle prized or ridiculed—
　　The vanity profound—

The laugh, or sigh, and changing hue—
The whisper, false or true—
Disdain, and triumph—such as fill
The world of pleasure still.
But one there was of happy mien,
Whom hour succeeding hour had seen
Await at Mina's side
A look, how long unconsciously denied!
But, when their glances met,
Could Mina then forget?
It seemed, her husband, present there
 In purer than his mortal prime,
Approached her from a higher sphere,
 Redeeming fate and time.
The ingenuous front—the ruddy brown,
Contending on his cheek with manhood's earliest down—
The quick, yet gentle eye—
The locks enwreathed of raven dye,
Crowning the form a king might wear—
 All, all were there.
  Nor these alone:
The same melodious eloquence of tone,
And every gesture aiding to express
The mental gracefulness.
And yet it was not he who died,
And still, alas! who claimed his mortal bride.

Ere her bewilderment had fled,
The cavalier addressed, and led
 His silent, unresisting choice
Where many a fair and noble Florentine
Expected him who gave the sign.
 O for an angel's voice
  To meet her ear!
To whisper once, " Forbear!"

And, with the music which awoke
    To guide the steps of sister art,
Perchance an angel spoke:
        It was no part
Of earthly melodist to cause
The solemn gentle sounds which sank at every pause.
    And Mina, not unused
To hymnings such as then she heard,
  Then only first refused
To welcome him they harbingered;
    Yet still his loved idea reigned
    Ev'n in the looks another gained.
But, when her yielded hand had filled
    The youth's enclasping hand,
A deeper cadence thrilled
    Among the tuneful band:
        Sullen it fell,
    Like sound of passing bell.
The vexed musician shook,
And eyed his fellows with reproachful look:
        They, only they,
Whose destiny was in the sound,
    Amid the general survey,
        In graceful round,
        Moved side by side,
Each with the other occupied.
They sped the fanciful career;
    Then, unresigning, tarried each,
    Hapless, in playful speech,
Which met, alas! a charméd ear;
And question and reply,
Impassioned rapidly,
Effused the glow on either cheek;
Nor yet they left to speak,

When, lo, the monitory sound again!
So loud, it hushed the tuneful strain.
   A sudden terror grew
In that disturbed society;
   And of the pausing few
Which was not forwardest to fly,
      One, one,
Where Mina listened, still remained—
Fond youth! and, when the tumult reigned,
   Mindful of her alone,
Essayed to clasp the spirit's bride.
A third alarum, iron-tongued, replied.
At its appalling sound
She turned, and gazed around.
Before her, in the mirror, shone
   The changeful light, the garish vest,
   Gathered around each flitting guest,
Reflected forms; and one
Whose image in the hall
   Was spectral all.
   It filled the space
Where she had almost met the youth's embrace—
A shade of lifeless hue,
And bore an import all too true
   To his offending bride,
While, sad and slow, he won her ear
With "Mina, I am here!"——
   She sank, and died.

And was there not a minister of light,[12]
   Who, that endurement o'er,
Winged heavenward his flight?
   The charge he bore
Was Mina's rescued soul—
His angel office, to control

The penitence which paid with life
　　A moment's mental perjury :
　　　To waft her to the sky,
　　　　The spirit wife
Of him who, in the realms of bliss,
　- Conveyed to her enraptured ear
Never more welcome sound than this—
　　" My Mina, I am here ! "

NOTES.

[1] *Alonzo the brave, and the fair Imogine.*
By the late M. G. Lewis, Esq.

A warrior so bold and a virgin so bright
   Discoursed as they sat on the green:
They gazed on each other with tender delight.
Alonzo the brave was the name of the knight,
   And the maid was the fair Imogine.

And "Ah!" said the youth, "since to-morrow I go
   To fight in a far distant land—
Your tears for my absence soon ceasing to flow,
Some other may court you, and you may bestow
   On a wealthier suitor your hand."

"Oh, hush these suspicions!" fair Imogine said,
   "Offensive to love and to me;
For if you be living, or if you be dead,
I swear, by the Virgin, that none in your stead
   Shall the husband of Imogine be.

"And if e'er I, by pride or by lust led aside,
   Forget thee, Alonzo the brave!
Heav'n grant that, to punish my falsehood and pride,
Thy ghost at my marriage may sit by my side,
May tax me with perjury, claim me as bride,
   And bear me away to the grave."

To Palestine hastened the hero so bold.
   His love, she lamented him sore:
But, scarce had a twelvemonth elapsed, when, behold!
A baron, bedizened with jewels and gold,
   Arrived at fair Imogine's door.

His beauty, his riches and ample domain,
   Soon made her untrue to her vows;
He dazzled her eyes, he bewildered her brain,
He caught her affections so light and so vain,
   And carried her home as his spouse.

And now had the marriage been blessed by the priest,
    The revelry now had begun;
The tables they groaned with the weight of the feast,
Nor yet had the laughter and merriment ceased,
    When the bell of the castle tolled "one."

'Twas then with amazement fair Imogine found
    That a stranger was placed by her side.
His air was terrific: he uttered no sound—
He spoke not—he moved not—he looked not around—
    But earnestly gazed on the bride.

His visor was closed, and gigantic his height;
    His armour was sable to view.
All pleasure and laughter were hushed at his sight;
The dogs, as they eyed him, drew back with affright,
    And the lights in the chamber burned blue.

His presence all bosoms appeared to dismay;
    Each guest sat in silence and fear.
At length said the bride, while she trembled, "I pray,
"Sir knight, that your helmet aside you would lay,
    And deign to partake of our cheer."

The lady is silent: the stranger complies—
    His helmet he slowly unclosed.
But, oh, what a sight met fair Imogine's eyes!
What words can express her dismay and surprise,
    When a skeleton's head is exposed!

All present then uttered a terrified shout,
    And turned in disgust from the scene;
The worms they crept in, and the worms they crept out,
And sported his eyes and his temples about,
    While the spectre addressed Imogine.

"Behold me, thou false one! behold me," he cried.
    "Remember Alonzo the brave.
Heav'n grants that, to punish thy falsehood and pride,
My ghost at thy marriage does sit by thy side,
Does tax thee with perjury, claim thee as bride,
    And bear thee away to the grave."

Thus saying, his arms round the lady he wound,
    While loudly she shrieked with dismay,
Then sank with his prey through the wide yawning ground;
Nor ever again was fair Imogine found,
    Nor the spectre who bore her away.

Not long lived the baron; and none, since that time,
   To inhabit the castle presume ;   .
For chronicles tell that, by order sublime,
There Imogine suffers the pains of her crime,
   And mourns her deplorable doom.

At midnight, four times in each year, doth her sprite,
   When mortals in slumbers are bound—
Arrayed in her bridal apparel of white,
Appear in the hall with the skeleton knight,
   And shriek as he clasps her around.

While they drink out of skulls newly torn from the grave,
   Dancing round them the spectres are seen ;
Their liquor is blood—and this horrible stave
They howl to the health of Alonzo the brave,
   And his consort the false Imogine.

PART I.

[2] *Where Arno wanders in his native plains.*

" The situation of Florence is singularly delightful. It stands in one of the most fertile plains, and on the margin of one of the most classic streams, in the world : at the base of the lofty chain of Apennines, which, sweeping round to the north, seem to screen it from the storms of winter ; while their sides, hung with chesnut woods, and their peaks, glittering with snow, rise far above the graceful slope and vine-covered height of Fiesole, whose utmost summit, crowned with a convent, half hid in a deep cypress grove, overlooks ' Florence the fair.' "

Rome in the 19th Century.

[3] *The temple of the Ausonian Muse.*

The Florentine Gallery.

[4] *Where sleep the Medicean race.*

"From this antechapel of tombs we entered the heavy and gloomy but most magnificent mausoleum of the Dukes of the Medici line. We passed unheeded the gorgeous monuments that fill its nitches ; but in the adjacent Church of San Lorenzo there was one tomb which arrested our steps and called forth our veneration. Here, beneath a plain flagstone, trodden by every foot, repose the ashes of Cosmo dè Medici, 'the Father of his Country.' This simple inscription, 'Patriæ Pater,.' conferred on him by the spontaneous gratitude of his fellow citizens, and more eloquent of praise than volumes of eulogium, is all that marks his unpretending grave. The memory of Cosmo dè Medici is written on a more durable monument than brass or marble —on the hearts of mankind, and in the impartial page of history."

ROME IN THE 19TH CENTURY.

[5] *Whence Buonaroti drew the immortal flame.*

"We visited with veneration the tomb of Michael Angelo Buonaroti; for, as Aretino said, 'the world has had many monarchs, but only one Michael Angelo.'

"It stands in the Church of Santo Cruce, and opposite to it is the monument of Galileo."

"It was here that the sister arts of painting, sculpture, and architecture, like the Graces, started at once into life, and, entwined in each other's arms, grew from infancy to maturity. It was here, after the slumber of ages, that divine poetry first reappeared upon earth —touched the soul of Dante with that inspiration which created a language harmonized by Heaven, and revealed to him in sublime visions of hell the horrors of the world to come, and to our own Milton, in glimpses of paradise, the beauty of that which was lost. It was here that infant science, beneath the fostering care of Galileo, disclosed her light to man."

IBID.

"Michael Angelo Buonaroti, a very celebrated painter, sculptor, and architect, born 1474, at Chiusi, a castle in the county of Arezzo, of a noble and ancient family descended from the Earls of Canoffe. Popes, kings, and grandees, and even Soliman, Emperor of the Turks, gave him public marks of their favour. This great artist died at Rome, 1564, aged 89. The Grand Duke, Cosmo dè Medici, had his corpse taken up in the night and carried to Florence."

COLLIGNON'S LADVOCAT'S DICTIONARY.

[6] *Or Galileo read the skies.*

"Galileo, natural son of Vincent Galilei, a noble Florentine, invented the telescope. By this instrument he first discovered Jupiter's four satellites, and made such discoveries in the heavens as will immortalize his name. He died at Florence, 1672, aged 78, having lost his sight three years before. Galileo invented the simple pendulum."

IBID.

7 *Or Dante pondered mysteries.*

" Dante Alighieri, one of the earliest and most celebrated Italian poets, born 1265, of a good family, at Florence, died in exile at Ravenna, 1321, aged 56. The principal among his poems is the poem of Hell, Purgatory, and Paradise."

IBID.

PART II.

8 *Of light and darkness to be felt;*
While images illusive flit
Before the vacant eye,
And tunes the changing chords emit
Are dissonance, not harmony.

" Even darkness which may be felt."

EXODUS, chap. x., ver. 21.

" For the elements were changed in themselves by a kind of harmony; like as, in a psaltery, notes change the name of a tune, and yet are always sounds."

WISDOM, chap. xix., ver. 18.

9 *The galliard.*

" An active, nimble, sprightly dance."

BACON.

" So stately his form, and so lovely her face,
That never a hall such a galliard did grace."

SCOTT'S LOCHINVAR. MARMION, canto 5.

10 *The joyous season of the Italian year.*

" The Carnival, properly speaking, begins after Christmas-day, and ends with the commencement of Lent: but it is only during the last eight days that masking is allowed in the streets;" " and when the bell of the capital, after midday, gives license for the reign of folly to commence, the most ridiculous figures issue forth." " The Corso is the scene of this curious revelry: the windows and balconies are hung with rich draperies, and filled with gaily dressed spectators. The little raised *trottoirs* by the side are set out with chairs, which are let and occupied by rows of masks. The street is, besides, crowded with pedestrians, masked and unmasked; and two rows of carriages, close behind each other, make a continual promenade."

" Both the masked and unmasked carry on the war by pelting each other with large handfuls of what ought to be comfits; but, these being too costly to be used in such profusion, they are actually no more than pozzelana, covered with plaster of Paris, and manufactured for this purpose under the name of *confitti de gesso* (plaster comfits). This coating flies off into lime dust, and completely whitens the figures of the combatants." "We sometimes received a discharge of real comfits; but they came like angel visits, few and far between." "Every day of the masquerade, the Corso becomes more crowded and more animated; till, on the last, the number and spirit of the masks, the skirmishes of sweetmeats and lime dust, and the shouts and ecstacies of all, surpass description."

ROME IN THE 19TH CENTURY.

[11] *Or gay festino filled the bright arcade.*

"There are only three festini, or public masked balls, allowed during the Carnival. They are held in the Teatro Alberto, a large handsome sala, now used only for this purpose. The stage and pit are open to the masks, and dancing of quadrilles, &c. goes on. The higher orders have boxes, and are generally unmasked; but in the course of the night they often walk about among the people, and mix with the motley crew."

IBID.

[12] *And was there not a minister of light?*

The conclusion of the Poem is suggested by a beautiful vignette, designed and placed by Lady Diana Beauclerk at the end of one of the translations of the German poem "Leonora," which her Ladyship's most graceful pencil had been doomed to illustrate by a succession of dismal and terrific images. Her feeling prompted her to conclude her task by the delineation of a beautiful seraph, bearing the rescued heart of the heroine to heaven.

The White Cat:

A FAIRY TALE.

PART I.

I vowed; and did a Muse allow
The poet, and receive his vow,
Beside the pure Castalian fountain—
 Where leaping, warbling, as it wells
Adown from the bi-crested mountain,[1]
 To Delphi's magic cells—
Around their glorious Godhead throng,
The choir of music and of song?

Th' ethereal courser—at whose dint [2]
The waters left their birth of flint—
With wings composed, and arching neck,
Awaits each tuneful sister's beck.
Whether Euterpe's breath inspire [3]
The flute, or Erato the lyre,
Or harp Terpsichore—their measures
From Clio drawing her historic treasures—
From bright Thalia comic glee—
Melpomene, thy tragic strain from thee—
Sweet eloquence in Polyhymnia's lay—
Urania's voice, that tells the starry way—
Calliope, thine epic line—
In all, and each, by turns, divine.

'Twas thus I vowed: "In mimic woe
From me no more shall numbers flow;
No more awake in mournful strain
The chord I will not strike again:

But I will utter pleasant rhymes,
For gentle ears, in sunny times.
My scenes shall be of hopeful spring,
Bright morn, and mayflower glistening.
My lovers shall be fair and sooth,
The course of their affection smooth;
The tyrant, in my song, shall fail,
The meek and virtuous prevail."

And Muses might have deigned 'agree
   To prosper this intention;
For then the poet's thought was free,
   And fertile his invention.
The hour which heard my votive song
Sleeps now, departed years among;
Eleven lustres are complete,
Imagination grown concrete,
   I cannot frame a tale.
From history or old romaunt
I must seek matter for my chaunt;
   Or, should their sources fail,
May peradventure fondly choose
From Mother Bunch or Mother Goose.

How rare are the riches of Fairyland dreams!
How frolic their mirth, and how wondrous their themes!
   What beauty and virtue adorn
Their heroes and heroines, gifted for good!
Yet elfin, accosted in petulant mood,
   May witch them to foul and forlorn.
My ears, even now, with astonishment tingle:
I follow an echo of fäery jingle:
Its quirks and its cadences give me a twist
Of fervour poetic I cannot resist.
I must, if Thalia will suffer me—what?
Take metrical license to sing " the White Cat."

The sun, which shed o'er fairy bowers
   His pale departing light,
But faintly glimmered on their flowers,
   And bade them sad good night.
Beyond, impervious to a ray,
   And girdling that enchanted ground,
A mighty forest lay,
   In vesper gloom profound.
Its thickets of primeval shade
Had formed a murky barricade,
Baffling at noon the gazer's eye;
   While other glades and banks were seen
   In radiance around serene.
And if, perchance, one ventured nigh,
Strange voices of unearthly tone,
Whistle and chirrup, sob and groan,
Impelled him from the haunted place
At headlong speed, with muffled face.

More savage now and deeper gloom
   Descends upon the wild—
Its forest branches shriek and boom,
   As if in ruin to be piled,
Prostrate beneath the rising squall.
Succeeds a voiceless interval,
Filled by the forkéd lightning's flash;
Then drops of rain in torrents dash,
And peals the thunderclap—its sound
Rattling and rolling on, around and yet around.
Stern hour, for youth so passing fair
As then was forced, on forest lair,
Amid the tempest, to aby
Such rugged hospitality!
His steed had fallen, worn with toil;
   Dispersed were all his train;

His cloak and plume besprent with soil,
    And moistened by the rain.
But yet his bright and glowing face
Relinquished not its highborn grace.
He thought upon his knightly oath;
More fondly, of his filial troth—
    And raised his head and smiled.
Uttered one silver bugle-call;
Listened, a moment's interval;
    Then plunged into the wild.

Youngest and gallantest of three
    Who graced a royal sire,
He wandered by a strange decree.
    This did the king require—
His sons in humble duty lent
Their troth to its accomplishment:—
"My sons, be mindful of the love
Your careful sire essays to prove:
Adventure for one year to find
A dog, most perfect of its kind.
Who brings it, shall ascend my throne,
Won by this duteous act alone."
Perhaps, to counsellors unjust
    The royal ear inclined;
Or jealousy awoke mistrust
    In his paternal mind.
He might esteem his power a boon
By young ambition sought too soon,
    And hesitate a space;
Or deem that pains and toil perchance
Would fit for his inheritance
    The worthiest of his race.
Perhaps the Fay Benevolent
Thus wrought, in aid of her intent

To render Prince Honorio blest,
Of power and wealth and love possessed;
And he had scarcely gained a rood
Within the mazes of the wood,
Brushing aside its bed of thorn,
When, lo! an answer to his horn—
With seven echoes, such as swell
Amid Killarney's mountain dell;
As perfect, with still pause between,
As if the waking voice had been
The music of a clarion's sound
From seven armaments around,
Each in its vale apart defying
By turns, and each by turns replying.
But, sooth to tell, these echoes spake
More plain than any of the lake.
Honorio's call had told the ear
A wildered knight alone was near.
The fairy answer came more full.
Witless were he who could not cull
From seven tones, in each a change,
Each than the last more sweet and strange,
Welcome, assurance, call to prove
Emprise, and faith, and hope, and love,
    And long and happy sway.
    He hastened to obey.
His spirit rose; his heart throbbed fast;
The forest glades were swiftly past.
Unwonted lustre fell between
The branches on the spangled green;
When, issuing from the fleckéd shade,
Honorio gained an esplanade,
    Some royal house before.
Its walls, transparent porcelain,
Were rich with many a coloured stain,
    Depicting fairy lore—   F

Legends of feat and merry things
   Which fays on earth had done;
And histories of all the kings
   Who filled an elfin throne.
The lofty portal glittered bright
With rays of self-emitted light
   From sapphires, set in gold;
   And, where the valves unrolled,
Depended from a diamond braid
A deer's foot, silver-laid.
Strange! thought Honorio, that the use
Of wealth and splendour so profuse
Is open to the spoiler's hand,
With none to question or withstand!
Fond youth! whoever seeks to find,
   When fairies favour not,
May range from Araby to Ind,
   And never gain the spot.
E'en then he seemed, as he advanced,
   To hear strange whisperings,
And feel the stir of many wings
   That in the vesper glanced;
As if, on that enchanted ground,
Unearthly warders held their round.
A moment at the door he stayed,
His hand upon the deer's foot laid,
   Before he pulled the chain:
His touch awoke melodious sound,
And hands of forms unseen around
   Retired the valves amain.
Twelve airy hands, in each a light,
Marshalled the footsteps of the knight.
A gentle touch upon his vest,
If e'er he paused, inviting pressed.
Again a melody was sung,
Of welcome, in the fairy tongue—

" Welcome, prince! no danger fear,
Mirth and love attend you here :
You shall break the magic spell
That on a beauteous lady fell.
Welcome, prince! no danger fear,
Mirth and love attend you here."

The gentle prince bore heart as brave
As hero of romance should have.
His was the glow of gen'rous zeal
To venture for a lady's weal;
Of trials best him listed those
In which the fairies interpose.
With less misgiving than surprise
   He trod at first th' enchanted ground;
   But when he heard his welcome sound,
His spirit sparkled in his eyes.
Courteous and unrestrained he stood,
   The charm of youthful grace
Immingling with the knightly mood
   Expressive in his face;
His falchion laid across his arm
In graceful bearing, not alarm.
Fair curls were blended with the down
   Of manhood on his cheek,
   And form and gesture seemed to speak
A gracefulness his own.
He trode upon a marquetry
Of lazuli and porphyry,
And passed within a coral gate
Self-opened into bowers of state,
Wondring at all that met his eyes,
   Rich, fanciful, and rare—
The fairest symmetries and dyes
   Of ocean, earth, and air;

Rich plume, and gem, and virgin ore,
And pearly shell, and madrepore;
And art, in all its bright array
For ease, enjoyment, and display;
And diamond rays, which fountains flung
Parterres of choicest flowers among;
And bright illuminations, shed
From thousand cressets o'er his head.

He was aware that at his side
The torch-filled hands had ceased to glide;
But others, fairer, seemed to wait
Upon his steps in duteous state,
The while from bower to bower he went,
In still increasing wonderment.
At length, a couch in chamber fair
    Moved forward to receive his form.
The hands exchanged, with ready care,
    His garments, wetted by the storm,
For dressing gown of rich brocade;
A toilet table moved to aid.
They hovered quickly o'er the couch,
Soliciting with gentlest touch
His stiffened limbs to suppleness,
And wringing moisture from each tress.
A golden censer glowed beneath
The molten perfume's spicy breath;
Above, the fragrant water rolled,
A tepid bath in font of gold.
Its service o'er, the prince, arrayed
    In stately vest of pall,
Was by the ready hands conveyed
    Within a splendid hall.
Two covers graced its regal board,
With rarest wines and viands stored.

He looked around the silent room—
Obeisance made, and said, " To whom
Is fortunate Honorio guest?"
The words were to himself addressed,
But answered by a voice at hand,
Melodiously sweet and bland ;
And, lo ! a little figure stood
Enwrapped in mourning veil and hood.
Two cats—a form feline they bore—
   With swords of state, were by her side,
And fifty cats of honour more
   In mute and graceful homage vied.
And yet it seemed their cattish sport
Accorded not with forms of court ;
For rats and mice, all sorts and ages,
Were borne by them in traps and cages.
With more of reverence than glee,
   Though both in turn prevailed,
Honorio bent his gentle knee
   Before the sable-veiled.
Her pages hastened to withdraw
Her hood and veil, with ready paw,
   And by his side she sat,
Upon an ottoman reclined—
Whitest and prettiest of her kind,
   But still, alas ! a cat.
And, " Welcome, Prince Honorio !" were
   Her words, in human tone ;
" A welcome simple and sincere
   Is thine, from maiden lone.
Lay toil and disappointment by,
And grace our hospitality ;
Nor marvel if, on fairy ground,
Things quaint and wonderful are found."

The splendour equalled not the taste
  With which the banquet was supplied,
Its rarest delicacies placed
  By hands at Prince Honorio's side.
His beauteous hostess supped apart—
  Pleased, interchanging converse fit
  With all the brilliancy, wit,
And aptitude of courtly art.
Strange! thought the prince, who heard her speak
  Like royal maiden nobly bred :
And what adventurer shall seek
  The clue to disentwine this thread ?
Her form is of the lower kind,
With human speech and princely mind !
Then polity, and maxims sage,
Such as were prized in former age—
The praise of chivalry, the glow
Which gen'rous hearts in triumph know,
The power of music and the lay
To win the raptured soul away—
All with such arguments approved
  As pure and cultured thoughts suggest,
And gentlest listeners have loved—
  Detained them till the hour of rest.
'Twas then he noticed that around
Her foot a tablet had been bound ;
Which, ere the timid foot withdrew,
Discovered to his eager view
A perfect semblance of himself,
Depicted by some skilful elf ;
And sure, it seemed, he could define
Expression almost feminine
In her averted cheek.
He faltered, and forbore to speak.

And now the dews of night descend; [4]
   The waning stars invite repose.
Reluctant, from his gentle friend
   Honorio to his chamber goes.
Rare plumage formed its tapestries,
   Embossed with wings of butterflies;
Its mirrors, ranged from floor to height,
Were lustrous with reflected light;
His couch was eider down, beneath
   The gauzes of a gay alcove,
Festooned by many a ribbon wreath
   Which elfin spinsters haply wove;
His duteous ministers, the hands,
Performed his toilet's last demands.
I tell not what Honorio chose
   For orison or vow,
When, sinking into sweet repose,
   He signed his breast and brow.
His Patron's aid, our Lady's grace,
Were prayer for knight in any case,
   And love had young Honorio none.
Perchance he vowed, were maiden kenned
With graces like his little friend,
   She would deserve his throne.

A pleasure more eager awoke with the morn.
   The dews, as they rose to the blue dappled skies,
   Left the redolent moisture which foresters prize,
And the courts echoed loud with the bugle and horn:
      Tralira! tralira! away!
There was halloo of huntsmen, and falconer's whoop,
Alluring his favourite tassel to stoop,
   And the deerhound immingled his bay.
To the prince, as he sprang from his pillow's embrace,
The hands had presented a habit for chace.

A collation was served ; and he saw in the court
Five hundred feline, who prepared for the sport:
   'Twas a festival day in the regions of fairy ;
And the white cat, his beautiful arbitress, came,
    Her black veil exchanged for a headdress more airy,
And prayed him to join in pursuit of the game.
Hand-ministers led a caparisoned steed—
Unmatched, she assured him, by zephyr, for speed.
For herself, on a frolicsome monkey she sat,
And clung to his neck with the grace of a cat.
The horns sounded lightly : tralira! away !
And when was there hunting more gallant and gay ?
The cats, as they ranged in the fairy preserves,
Made a mewing would flutter the steadiest nerves.
They ran twice as fast as the rabbits and hares,
Which they caught in their clutches or drove into snares;
Then brought them *en battue* the white cat before,
And exhausted each antic of game-catching lore.
But their feats were by those of the monkey surpassed:
With the white cat *en croupe*, like Gäifros he passed.[5]
By him were the loftiest trees escaladed,
The haunts of the squirrel and eaglet invaded.
In vain barked poor scug, and tossed pertly his fruit
At the foes whom he strove to deter from pursuit;
In vain clamoured eaglet, and hovered on high
The shadow parental, obscuring the sky :
Both squirrel and eaglet were borne to the green
Where the cat-court awaited their beautiful queen.
'Twas then the white cat, with the natural grace
Befitting a dame of superior race,
   Accosted the prince at her side.
" Thus far, gentle guest, you have witnessed and shared
The sports by our spell-bounden lieges prepared,
   And such as our marvellous fortunes provide.
Let it now be your part to pursue unrestrained
   The pleasures of Fairyland hunting awhile :

Your courser and hounds have been gallantly trained,
  For courage and speed are unmatched in our isle;
And some, who attend you unseen, will be found
Expert in the choice of your covert and ground.
By the woodside I wait you. Success to your sport!
Be your pastime complete, and our severance short."

Honorio proffered his graceful adieu,
  And turned his bright steed to the covert amain.
  The deerhounds obeyed an invisible train,
Who led them across the broad champaign in view.
They sped over fern hills, and thickets among,
And at intervals challenged with dubious tongue,
Till a stag of the boldest, aroused from his lair,
  Leaped forth in the sight of the forwardest hound;
  The park to his baying responded around,
And bugle and shout echoed far in the air.
High mantled the blood in Honorio's face;
  He pressed his brave steed with a sportsman's delight,
Sustained his career at the head of the chase,
  And kept the magnificent quarry in sight.
Long, long, in his vigour, disdained the bold stag
  To double, or veer from a foe yet afar;
He scorned all advantage of forest or crag
  While the plain rang behind him with impotent war,
But held over moorland, and champaign, and hill,
Pursued by the youthful Honorio still.
He faltered at length, for his forces declined;
  His chest and his shoulders were flecked with spray;
His breathing came thickened with sobs on the wind,
  And near and more near pealed the clamour and bay.
A moment he lowered to windward his ear,
  As he caught his pursuers' reply;
Then gathered his haunches in midmost career,
  Aware that a spot for retreating was nigh,

And sprang through a cleft in the mountain's red breast,
Escaped from the view, and perhaps from the quest.
The covert he chose for concealment was apt;
A rocky ravine, by the wavy clouds capt,
　And closed by a barrier of stone.
Escape was afforded alone at the foot,
Where, spangling the pebbles and alder's gray root,
　A sparkle of water there shone.
Full soon the bold cry, which had languished a space,
　Was borne on the breezes anew,
And the forms of his foes round his tarryingplace
　Drew forth the beleaguered to view.
He stood like a monarch, impatient to fly:
　His nostrils were spread in disdain;
Dark flashed the fell glance from his blood-rolling eye,
　And aback shrank the fear-stricken train.
The voice of Honorio, the shouting around,
　Had hardly recalled them to bay,
When he burst through the pack with a desperate bound,
　And won to the water his way.
Its devious margin eluded the glance;
　But the wave rippled lucidly clear,
And a fairy barge glided along its expanse
　To receive the discomfited deer.
Extended were hands from the gaily trimmed stern,
　And cheered an invisible crew,
While they crowned the bold stag with a garland of fern,
　And bore him to hunting grounds new.
And then the recall, with its musical swell
　That slowly and sweetly expired,
Rang over the water, and valley, and fell,
　While the prince from his pastime retired.

Again the pleasant evening, banquet-crowned,
　And occupied in converse of delight,
With intervals of song or music' sound,

Stole softly on the placid hours of night.
And while Honorio bent, with captive ear,
   O'er that small form, recumbent at his side,
And felt a wondrous hope, restrained by fear,
   Like lover wooing his affianced bride;
And, while he strove for very shame
   With all his wit to disintwine
The spell which bound a peerless dame
   Within the form feline;
What marvel that his sire's behoof
Was like to fail of filial proof—
That, when the year had almost ended,
The prize on which a throne depended
   Was still unfound, unsought,
While he, possessed with happier thought,
Remained a guest in fairy cell,
Sans wish or power to bid farewell?
'Twas then his faithful friend repaid
His gen'rous care with elfin aid.
" My prince," she said, " the boon I give
   Demands but faith in him receiving;
Then, let the trial hour arrive,
   The prize will rest with the believing.
Within this acorn is confined
A dog, most perfect of its kind."
Honorio bent his ear, and, hark!
An echo of a fairy bark!

And now such interval as drew
The friends towards their first adieu
   Was pleasurably passed.
No, promise was received or claimed,
No season of returning named,
   When came farewell at last;
For either seemed alike impressed
   With hope so sweet and sure—

Such happy sunshine of the breast,
  In mutual faith secure—
That sorrow, with her dim control,
Upon their parting never stole.
" Where are the sports I lately led?
How soon, yet not for ever, fled!"
  Might Prince Honorio say;
While, to his faithful steed addressed,
The fairy present at his breast,
  He bent to court his way.

PART II.

Another fled, and waned another year,
And then Honorio's final task was near.
Already, twice, the lingerer
   Had sighed to leave th' enchanted dame,
And wended homewards to prefer
   An owned but unrequited claim.
His acorn had, in sooth, confined
A dog, most perfect of its kind,
   To which the recompense was due.
But, still, reluctant to resign
His throne to any of his line,
   Their sire proposed a trial new.
He praised their piety and zeal,
But met them with a new appeal.
"Adventure for another year;
And then before our throne appear,
Producing each a web of lawn
That through a needle can be drawn.
I yield the prize to his success
Whom, then, his destiny shall bless."

Again the prince had hastened to his friend—
   Told of his speed, and next appointed token:
Again the waning year approached its end,
   Their faith fast plighted, and the spell unbroken.
A walnut was her parting gift,
Provided for his hour of shrift ;

This, when his finger pierced the shell,
Disclosed a filbert in its cell.
Each courtier's smile, and rival's tone,
   Urged Prince Honorio to proceed:
The filbert bore a cherry stone,
   The kernel wheat, its grain a millet seed.
Ah, faithless friend! he thought: then found
   A cat-touch o'er his finger drawn,
And from the millet seed unwound
   A wondrous length of lawn,
Four hundred yards, of rainbow dye,
Which passed with ease the needle's eye.
Again was his the triumph; and again,
It seemed, his patience and success were vain.
Reluctance, in the royal breast,
   Was mixed with thought perhaps like shame,
While thus again the king addressed
   The rival princes of his name—
"Another year, and then approach our side;
My throne is his who leads the loveliest bride!"

Honorio hastened to the cell
   With sad but undivided heart—
"My heritage, my throne, farewell!"
   He cried; "for never will I part
With one so dear, so fondly tried,
   For royal dower or peerless bride.
Oh, were thy benefits forgot,
   Thy pure and graceful mind,
Thy cruel and mysterious lot,
   Within that form confined;
Yet I have vowed to set thee free,
Or share thy destiny with thee."
Kind, but yet grave, was her reply;
It seemed to veil a mystery.

Again her hospitable care
Bade fairy ministers prepare
The song, the banquet, and the sport;
Again the waning year grew short,
How swiftly passed! but not for these—
E'en fairy sports had ceased to please.
For pastime vain was converse sweet
 Between th' enchanted and her guest;
As when some youth and maiden meet,
 With mutual love impressed.
But admiration of a mind
Like hers accomplished and refined
Was mingled with awakening grief
When, now, the allotted time grew brief.
'Twas not thy part, Honorio, now
 To have forgotten, and to hear,
By her reminded, of thy filial vow,
 And of the waning year.
It was not thine to meet her aid,
Now first unwontedly delayed;
But, after expectation vain,
In fond despondence to complain.
Thine utterance dissolved a spell,
As many a maiden knows full well-
Who has to falter, ere approve
The vow breathed forth from lips of love.
" With thee, my prince, our rescue lies,
And this the hour! be firm, be wise!"

She spoke, and led the way alone
 Through gallery and colonnade.
The fairy splendours faintly shone,
 The beauty seemed to fade;
An odour of expiring flowers
Breathed over her voluptuous bowers.

She passed the scenes of loveliness
Her feet were ne'er again to press,
And gained a portal unexplored:
Honorio followed with his sword.
Gates, self-evolved, with awful din
  Admitted heroine and knight,
And, when their shadows shrank within,
  Reclosed, by necromantic might.
Echoes unearthly seemed to meet
The fall of their advancing feet.
Their way was traced by Runic lines;
  And many-coloured flame,
Along the characters and signs,
  By fits retired and came.
Honorio thought but of his vow;
  He recked not sound nor sight;
His cheeks were warmed with virtuous glow,
  His eyes with sparkles bright;
The spirit of his hundred sires
Inflamed his heart with noble fires:
But not in his enchanted path
  An adversary rose,
Such as the steel-armed warrior hath
  Amid a field of foes.
A figure, in the form feline,
With gesture bland and look benign,
  Went forth his steps before:
She heeded not the unearthly sound,
Nor feared to tread the mystic ground
  Those lambent flashes wore.
And now the fires, converging, rose
  In pyramidic stream,
Such as an opening fountain throws
  Across the sunny beam;
Emitting rays of every hue,
Vermilion, crysolite, and blue.

The showers of their ascending light
Cleft not the canopy of night
   Which overhung the spot;
And vapour dense, that rose aloof,
Repelled them from the unfathomed roof
   Of that enchanted grot.
An altar-stone across was laid,
And here the white conductress stayed.
" It was a pleasant office, mine,
To welcome guest of royal line
Within my bowers," she said, "awhile
His weary trials to beguile,
And aid him to deserve success;
What lady would adventure less?
And, were Honorio vain and cold,
His thanks had gallantly been told,
My passing courtesies repaid,
And free the gentle prince had strayed;
Albeit, t'were hard to disintwine
The chain which binds my lot with thine.
But thou wert generous, and prompt
To render for my cares accompt
Of thankfulness above their due;
And from that recognition grew
The wish, and then the choice, to aid—
As yet unclaimed and unessayed.
Now I beseech thee, burst my chains!
The rest with destiny remains.
Do thou, in faith of knighthood pure,
Vow to perform what I adjure.
With thee alone my rescue lies,
And this the hour!"   The prince replies,
" Thou never canst adjure for ill:
In faith of knighthood pure—I will!"
She answered, " When I press this stone,
Unloose the falchion from thy zone;

Let neither doubt nor fear prevail:
Deprive me of my head and tail,
And bid them feed the streams of fire
That in this mystic grot aspire."

As one upon volcano's brink,
Honorio felt his spirit sink.
Regard, humanity, forbade;
And yet, alas! his vow was made,
That altar-stone already pressed.
In misery he manned his breast.
Twice, while his power and sense remained,
His sword was wielded and regained,
The precious relics it divided
To those ascending flames confided,
   And motionless Honorio lay.
It was a light but thrilling touch
That called him from his stony couch
   To scene of happier day.
He looked, and, lo! a lady, bright
As denizen from realm of light,
   Inclined on him her sweet regard.
She bore a royal diadem,
And sceptre, rich with many a gem:
   These formed not his reward.
It was her look of grateful love,
And meek devotedness, above
   Her youthful beauty's power:
Yet she was fair as poets feign
Some goddess of Olympus' reign,
   Or Cytharæan bower,
Such as adventurer of old
Had traversed empires to behold.
Where was Honorio? bending low
   In lover's transport at her feet;
And destined, when he told his vow,

To listen to these accents sweet—
"All, all, my prince most true and brave!
That thou dost win and merit, have,
   Our royal hand and throne;
And all affection to her lord
That plighted lady can accord
   Is thine, and thine alone."

Some moments—and the hand which joined
His hand and lip had been resigned.
When Prince Honorio gazed around,
No more they trod enchanted ground:
   Of all the fairy charm,
The tablet which his form impressed
Alone remained—'twas at her breast,
   Its chain upon her arm.
"Behold! where ocean joys to lave,
Enamoured, with his brightest wave,
   Six kingdoms, famed of yore:
Thee Gloriana, queen of all,
Bids welcome to her fathers' hall,
   And to her native shore.
Her lot "——Here paused the royal fair;
For, lo! a shout which filled the air,
A long and gratulating sound,
Was echoed round and yet around;
And dames and nobles of her race
Compressed in dutiful embrace
Her hand, her royal robe, and knees:
Those from her palace hurrying; these,
With her, from fairy penance freed
By Prince Honorio's happy deed.
She raised and kissed them one by one;
Then, with the affianced of her throne,
Rejoicing, up the proud ascent,
Amid their gratulations, went.   G 2

Soon there was fit occasion found
  In Prince Honorio's ear to tell
(He promised secresy profound)
Wherefore his princess had been bound
  In form.feline, by fairy spell.
But, though to lady of romance,
Redeemed from such unhappy chance,
All proper deference is due,
And ev'ry word, I know, was true;
I found the tale so very dull,
My Muse repeats it not in full.
Suffice it, having chanced to pain
  An ancient fairy, rather cross,
She was condemned, with all her train,
  To suffer of their persons loss;
And, had not Fay Benevolent
Contrived to end their punishment
With aid of Prince Honorio's sword,
Their forms had never been restored.

It was the matin hour in lovely spring;
The latest star was faintly glimmering;
The golden sunrise softened by the dew,
And heaven above an arch of cloudless blue;
The vernal landscape and the wave were bright,
And all around a promise of delight: .
Yet all was still, save for the thrush's tale,
And voice of flock and herd in distant vale.
The peasant went not on his early way,
The little villagers forbore to play,
And maid and matron were alike unseen
In blooming orchard or on flow'ry green.
All hastened to the royal towers,
  Expecting pomp and holiday;
For Avalonia's gallant powers [1]

Were gathered there in proud array :
They kept the lofty folded gate,
And heavy drawbridge raised for state.
Above, around, in equal row,
The marksmen bent the ready bow,
And flash of golden panoply
From knightly cohort glittered by.
The turreted and curtained mound,
 Saluted earliest by the sun,
Was wakened from repose profound
 By festival begun,
And banderol and pennon fair
Were spread upon the morning air;
 And, over all, unrolled
Thine impress, Gloriana, bright—
A bird which poised its wings for flight
 Amid a field of gold.

Then through the unfolded portals came
The powers of many a noble name—
 Each bore their leader's cognizance;
And, distant first and then more near,
Light music fell upon the ear
 That watched their prompt advance.
Who, that had viewed them, as they came
With open brow and sturdy frame,
And lively eye, serene and proud,
That glanced among the busy crowd,
But had exulted to have known
Their martial service for his own?
But there was pomp of loftier grace
Along the flower-besprinkled space
Where thronged the chivalry to view
 Their lately rescued queen;
And, as the royal escort drew
 Their noble ranks between,

Kissed and unclosed each steelclad hand,
And dropped its gauntlet on the sand,
Defying Christendom to fight
In peerless Gloriana's right.
And there were beauteous forms attending,
From palfrey or from litter bending,
With many a glance and many a smile,
And hand and kerchief waved the while;
And frequent voice of beauteous dame,
Hushed only when the sovereign came.
Eight milkwhite steeds, of matchless race,
    Were harnessed to her moving throne;
Her side was Prince Honorio's place,
    He gazed on her alone.
A diamond sceptre of command
Was clasped within her purer hand;
Her hair, enwreathed and gemmed, was pressed
    By Avalonia's crown of gold;
A falling veil escaped her vest,
    And hung upon her mantle's fold.
Whom then her glance of beauty met,
    Her softened and delighted air,
Had they not taught him to forget
    That any but herself was fair?
And who in ev'ry look had viewed
    Expression pure and kind,
And guessed not the beatitude
    Within her heart enshrined?
In sooth, a guardian undiscovered
That morning o'er her couch had hovered.
'Twas there the Fay Benevolent
In smiling gratulation bent;
All happy influences wrought,
    And all unlovely chased away;
She there inspired the dreamer's thought
    To meet the triumph of the day,

And whispered promise of success
To her awakened loveliness—
Fair seas around her galley's prow,
   Light airs to waft her o'er the main
   And hasten her return again,
 And blessings on her nuptial vow;
And then, a fairy kiss, impressed
On either cheek, dispelled her rest;
And, lo! the guardian form ascended
In smiles, wherewith a tear was blended.
Oh, never, from her natal day,
   Had Gloriana lovelier been,
Than when the vision passed away,
   And rose th' enraptured queen—
Her cheek with all its influence glowing,
Her hair in artless ringlets flowing,
Her gesture and her step elate;
And, lo! upon the couch of state,
A wreath of myrtle flowers left,
And wondrous veil of fairy weft!

And now, her escort turned to gain
   The water-margent sand,
Closed by a long and brilliant train.
   The royal barge was manned.
Garments or tapestries before [2]
   Her gentle footsteps spread,
As she descended to the shore,
   By Prince Honorio led.
The joy which reverence had sealed,
Burst then, by look and lip revealed.
The crowd acclaimed; the minstrels sang,
   And tuned their most triumphant lays;
And ocean to the horizon rang
   With Gloriana's praise.

Now sail and streamer caught the wind.;
And in their bark of state reclined,
The queen and her affianced knew
That fairy promises were true:
For never, since the time of yore,
When Argo left the Colchian shore,
　Was galley half so free and light
As this, careering on its way
By tower and headland, port and bay,
　Six glorious realms in sight.

Honorio's ardent smile, as he beheld
The bark upon his native shore propelled,
Drew blushes from the silent queen,
Behind her fairy veil unseen.
And now the destined port was neared;
The royal hail received and cheered.
A noble troop were gathering
To meet and lead them to the king;
And Gloriana touched the land,
Supported by Honorio's hand.
His brothers twain, a princely pair,
With each a dame of lovely air,
　Awaited his caress;
For theirs was contest frank and free,[3]
Affection equal in degree,
　And all ingenuousness.

As wonted, to the palace came,
Full of the tidings, gossip fame.
The royal mind was strangely fluttered—
Some indistinct conclusions uttered.
With wondrous speed, the monarch bade
His pages have his throne arrayed—

Met and enfolded in his arms
His princely sons and ev'ry bride—
Then sat in judgment to decide
　Upon the ladies' charms;
And, as undoubted legends own,
Upon some plea to keep his throne.

In order of their birth arose
　His sons, and sought their father's side,
Each in impatience to disclose
　The beauties of his bride.
The veils of twain had been withdrawn,
And courtiers hailed the lovely dawn
Behind those snowy tissues peeping,
And there were dames for envy weeping,
When Prince Honorio, calm but pale,
　Impressed on Gloriana's hand
　A kiss, and prayed her give command
To disengage her veil.
It fell: the fairy task was done.
Breathed ever maiden lovelier?　None.
The assembly saw the monarch's gaze
With murmur unrepressed of praise.
Would not his royal crown be brought—
　The glorious prize, by beauty won,
　Descend upon his happiest son?
Such was not Gloriana's thought.
Observant of the last behest.
　Of Fay Benevolent, that morn,
She spoke, while ev'ry look expressed
How noblest thoughts with kindest strove—
How maidenness and happy love
　By beauteous majesty were worn:—
" Great king, what pity to demit
An office for yourself most fit!

More pity, to misdeem that those,
   Nearest in duty as in place,
Would cherish thought to interpose
   Between your people and your grace!
Too soon your sceptre will be won,
When fate permits your chosen son
To bear it to some future age,
As his paternal heritage.
For me my fortune had ordained
Six realms, o'er which my father reigned:
To Prince Honorio's faith I owe
More than all empire can bestow.
Permit us to divide our states
   Of hexarchy among your line;·
For either prince a kingdom waits—
   Honorio's bridal gift, and mine.
And deign to bless our nuptial vows"
   (And then in filial act she bent).
   The happy monarch sobbed assent.
"And, while the fav'ring breeze allows,
Permit to seek our realms again,
And order the fraternal reign."
Then, with a soft and playful smile
(The princely lovers knelt around,
In speechless gratitude profound)—
"Your majesty may please awhile
   The award of beauty to defer.
Present are three that have their choice;
And each, perhaps, one partial voice
   That would assign the palm to her."

A tale is nought without a moral.
   This was Calliope's decree;
And her award, in answer choral,
   Assented to by sisters three.[4]

This tale has moral—who can miss it?
Wits may aver, and is not this it?
When tempests lower and evening closes,
Knights errant! follow your own noses!
Approach all palaces, invited;
Leave never female favour slighted;
And pay for what fair dames accord
And you accept, at point of sword.
Bright heroines! be circumspect,
And treat not fairies with neglect:
Or, having slighted their advice,
Be for the future most precise;
For, of all *gouvernantes*, they
Reward you best, if you obey.
And, in event of your succeeding,
Behave with kindness and good breeding.

But I have moral more refined,
For hearers of a gentler mind.
Which are the fays of happiest power
  To guard and guide a youthful friend—
Which, to dispense the richest dower,
  To those that on their aid depend?
Is not each good and humble thought
  Conceived and cherished in the soul,
The fairy by whose power is wrought
  Obedience, virtue, self-control—
The genius by whose guidance pure
Our happiness becomes secure?
'Twas thus in young Honorio grew
  Resolve so fair, from filial love;
From gratitude, affection true—
  And faith, impediments above;
And, with reward of power and fame,
Ability to grace them came.

Nor fear, if Fortune wave her wings,[5]
   That false and cruel arbitress!
Your fairies bring you better things
   Than power, and riches, and success—
The will from virtue never swerving,
The consciousness of well deserving,
And peace, and general esteem,
And all that wise men treasures deem.

   Ye lovely listeners! receive,
     Like Gloriana, trials dure:
Your fairies do not idly grieve,
     They try you but to reassure.
Losing, be ready to despise
     All that your better thoughts refuse;
Winning, remember that your prize
     Derives its value from its use.

And of the Salamancans twain [6]
     From margin of the fountain gone—
That, bootless, on his road again;
   This, rich in treasure from the stone—
Each be the last, and bear away
     The moral of my tale of fay.

NOTES.

PART I.

1 *The bi-crested mountain.*

" Parnassus, a mountain of Greece, gives source to several streams, particularly the Castalian spring, which issues from a chasm between two lofty summits of a precipice one hundred feet high, and thence descends to Delphi."

GAZETTEER.

2 *Th' ethereal courser.*

Pegasus.

3 *Whether Euterpe's breath inspire*
The flute.

" History was assigned to Clio, tragedy to Melpomene, comedy to Thalia, the flute to Euterpe, the harp to Terpsichore, the lyre and the lute to Erato, epic poetry to Calliope, astronomy to Urania, and rhetoric to Polyhymnia."

LADVOCAT.

4 *And now the dews of night descend.*

" Et jam nox humida cœlo
Præcipitat, suadentque cadentia sidera somnos."

VIRG., Æn. II.

5 *With the white cat en croupe, like Gäifros he passed.*

" That there figure on horseback, wrapped up in a cloak of Gascony, is the very individual Don Gayferos, to whom his own lady, by this time, revenged of the presumptuous and enamoured Moor, talks with more seeming composure from the battlements of the tower, supposing him to be some traveller. You see how Gayferos discovers himself, and learn from the joyful gestures of Melisendra that she recognizes her husband; especially as we now see her let herself down from the balcony, in order to get on horseback behind her spouse: but, as ill luck would have it, the border of her under petticoat has caught hold of the iron spikes of the balcony; and there she hangs, dangling, without being able to reach the ground. But you see how compassionate Heaven brings relief in the most pressing emergencies; for Don Gayferos comes to her assistance, and, without minding whether or not the rich petticoat may be torn, seizes his lady, and by main force brings her to the ground: then, with one jerk, sets her upon the crupper of his horse astride like a man, bidding her hold fast and throw her arms around his neck so as to cross them on his breast, that she may be in no danger of falling."

SMOLLETT'S DON QUIXOTE, Part II., B. 2, chap. ix.

PART II.

[1] *Avalonia's gallant powers.*

Avalonia, the title here given to the principal kingdom of the disenchanted princess, included a cluster of hills anciently called the island of Avalon, now part of Somersetshire, surrounded by a flat pastoral country of considerable extent, which is bounded on the north by the Mendip, on the south by Poledown and other hills, on the west by the Bristol Channel, and on the east by the hills on the borders of Wiltshire.

[2] *Garments or tapestries before*
Her gentle footsteps spread.

The gallant and unfortunate Sir Walter Raleigh first attracted the notice of Queen Elizabeth by casting his cloak before her as she was passing some miry ground in her progress from her palace at Greenwich to the Thames.

[3] *For theirs was contest frank and free.*

When Charles the Fifth and Francis the First were candidates for the imperial crown—"We both court the same mistress," said Francis, with his usual vivacity; "each ought to urge his suit with all the address of which he is master. The most fortunate will prevail, and the other must rest contented."

ROBERTSON.

[4] *Assented to by sisters three.*

To whom the manuscript was first read.

[5] *Nor fear if Fortune wave her wings,*
That false and cruel arbitress!

"Fortuna, sævo læta negotio, et
    Ludum insolentem ludere pertinax,

Transmutat incertos honores,
　Nunc mihi, nunc alii benigna.
Laudo manentem.　Si celeres quatit
Pennas, resigno quæ dedit, et meâ
　Virtute me involvo, probamque
　　Pauperiem sine dote quæro.

Hor., Od. xxix., lib. 3.

[6] *The Salamancans twain.*

"Gil Blas, au Lecteur :

"Avant que d'entendre l'histoire de ma vie, écoute, ami lecteur, au conte que je vais te faire.

"Deux écoliers alloient ensemble de Penafiel à Salamanque. Se sentant las et altérés, ils s'arrêterent au bord d'une fontaine, qu'ils rencontrèrent sur leur chemin.　Là, tandis qu'ils se délassaient, après s'être désaltérés, ils apperçurent, par hazard, auprès d'eux, sur une pierre à fleur de terre, quelques mots, déjà un peu effacés par le temps, et par les pieds des troupeaux qu'on venoit alreuver à cette fontaine.　Ils jettèrent de l'eau sur la pierre pour la laver, et ils lurent ces paroles Castillanes—'Aqui esta encerrada el alma del Licenciado Pedro Garcias.'　('Ici est enfermée l'âme du Licencie Pierre Garcias.')

"Le plus jeune des écoliers, qui étoit vif et étourdi, n'eut pas achevé de lire l'inscription, qu'il dit, en riant de toute sa force, 'Rien n'est plus plaisant !　'Ici est enfermée l'âme'!　Une âme enfermée !　Je voudrois scavoir quel original a pu faire une si ridicule epitaphe.'　En achevant ces paroles, il se leva pour s'en aller.　Son compagnon, plus judiceux, dit en lui-même, 'Il y a là dessous quelque mystère.　Je veux demeurer ici pour l'eclaircir.'　Celui-ci laissa donc partir l'autre, et, sans perdre de temps, se mit à creuser avec son couteau tout autour de la pierre.　Il trouva dessous une bourse de cuir, qu'il ouvrit.　Il y avoit dedans cent ducats, avec une carte, sur laquelle étoient écrites ces paroles, en Latin—'Sois mon héritier, toi qui as eu assez d'esprit pour démêler le sens de l'inscription; et fais un meilleur usage que moi de mon argent.'　L'écolier, ravi de cette découverte, remit la pierre comme elle étoit auparavant, et reprit le chemin de Salamanque avec l'âme du licencié.

"Qui que tu sois, ami lecteur, tu vas ressembler à l'un ou à l'autre de ces deux écoliers.　Si tu lis mes aventures sans prendre garde aux instructions morales quelles renferment, tu ne tireras aucun fruit de cet ouvrage; mais si tu le lis avec attention, tu y trouveras, suivant le précepte d'Horace, l'utile mêlé avec l'agréable."

Le Sage, Preface to "Gil Blas."

THE WHITE CAT.

A Fairy Tale.

THERE was once a king who had three sons, all remarkably hand-some in their persons, and in their tempers brave and noble. Some wicked courtiers made the king believe that the princes were im-patient to wear the crown, and that they were contriving a plot to deprive him of his sceptre and his kingdom. The king felt he was growing old, but, as he found himself as capable of governing as he had ever been, he had no inclination to resign his power; and therefore, that he might pass the rest of his days peaceably, he de-termined to employ the princes in such a manner as at once to give each of them the hope of succeeding to the crown, and fill up the time they might otherwise spend in so undutiful a manner.

He sent for them to his cabinet, and, after conversing with them kindly, he added, " you must be sensible, my dear children, that my great age prevents me from attending so closely as I have hitherto done to State affairs. I fear this may be injurious to my subjects; I therefore desire to place my crown on the head of one of you: but it is no more than just that, in return for such a present, you should procure me some amusement in my retirement, before I leave the capital for ever. I cannot help thinking that a little dog that is handsome, faithful, and engaging, would be the very thing to make me happy; so that, without bestowing a preference on either of you, I declare that he who brings me the most perfect little dog shall be my successor."

The princes were much surprised at the fancy of their father, to have a little dog, yet they accepted the proposition with pleasure; and accordingly, after taking leave of the king, who presented them with abundance of money and jewels, and appointed that day twelve-month for their return, they set off on their travels.

Before taking leave of each other, they took some refreshment to-gether in an old palace about three miles out of town, where they mutually agreed to meet in the same place on that day twelvemonth, and go altogether with their presents to court. They also agreed to change their names, that they might be unknown to everyone in their travels.

Each took a different road; but it is intended to relate the adventures of only the youngest, who was the handsomest, most amiable, and accomplished prince that had ever been seen. No day passed, as he travelled from town to town, that he did not buy all the handsome dogs that fell in his way; and, as soon as he saw one that was handsomer than those he had before, he made a present of the last, for twenty servants would have been scarcely sufficient to take care of all the dogs he was continually buying. At length, wandering he knew not whither, he found himself in a forest; night suddenly came on, and with it a violent storm of thunder, lightning, and rain. To add to this perplexity, he lost his path, and could find no way out of the forest. After he had groped about for a long time, he perceived a light, which made him suppose he was not far from some house; he accordingly pursued his way towards it, and, in a short time, found himself at the gates of the most magnificent palace he had ever beheld. The door that entered into it was made of gold, covered with sapphire stones, which cast so resplendent a brightness over everything around, that scarcely could the strongest eyesight bear to look at it: this was the light the prince had seen from the forest. The walls of the building were of transparent porcelain, variously coloured, and represented the history of all the fairies that had existed from the beginning of the world. The prince, coming back to the golden door, observed a deer's foot fastened to a chain of diamonds: he could not help wondering at the magnificence he beheld, and the security in which the inhabitants seemed to live; "for," said he to himself, "nothing can be easier than for thieves to steal this chain, and as many of the sapphire stones as would make their fortunes."

He pulled the chain, and heard a bell, the sound of which was exquisite. In a few moments the door was opened; but he perceived nothing but twelve hands in the air, each holding a torch. The prince was so astonished that he durst not move a step; when he felt himself gently pushed on by some other hands from behind him. He walked on in great perplexity till he entered a vestibule inlaid with porphyry and lapis stone, where the most melodious voice he had ever heard chanted the following words:—

H

" Welcome, prince! no danger fear,
Mirth and love attend you here;
You shall break the magic spell
That on a beauteous lady fell.
Welcome, prince! no danger fear,
Mirth and love attend you here."

The prince now advanced with confidence, wondering what these words could mean. The hands moved him forward to a large door of coral, which opened of itself to give him admission into a splendid apartment built of mother-of-pearl, through which he passed into others so richly adorned with paintings and jewels, and so resplendently lighted with thousands of lamps, girandoles, and lustres, that the prince imagined he must be in an enchanted palace.

When he had passed through sixty apartments, all equally splendid, he was stopped by the hands: a large easy chair advanced of itself to the chimney; and the hands, which he observed were extremely white and delicate, took off his wet clothes and supplied their place with the finest linen imaginable, and then added a commodious wrapping gown, embroidered with the brightest gold, and all over enriched with pearls. The hands next brought him an elegant dressing table, and combed his hair so very gently that he scarcely felt their touch. They held before him a beautiful basin filled with perfumes, for him to wash his face and hands, and afterwards took off the wrapping gown and dressed him in a suit of clothes of still greater splendour. When his dress was complete, they conducted him to an apartment he had not yet seen, and which also was magnificently furnished. There was in it a table spread for a repast, and everything upon it was of the purest gold, adorned with jewels. The prince observed there were two covers set, and was wondering who was to be his companion, when his attention was suddenly caught by a small figure not a foot high, which just then entered the room and advanced towards him. It had on a long black veil, and was supported by two cats, dressed in mourning, with swords by their sides. They were followed by a numerous retinue of cats, some carrying cages full of rats, and others mouse-traps full of mice.

The prince was at a loss what to think. The little figure now approached, and, throwing aside her veil, he beheld a most beautiful white cat. She seemed young and melancholy; and, addressing herself to the prince, she said, " Young prince, you are welcome; your presence affords me the greatest pleasure." " Madam," replied the prince, " I would fain thank you for your generosity; nor can I help observing, that you must be an extraordinary creature, to possess with your present form the gift of speech, and the magnificent palace I have seen." " All this is very true," answered the beautiful cat; " but, prince, I am not fond of talking, and least of all do I like compliments; let us therefore sit down to supper." The trunkless hands then placed the dishes on the table, and the prince and the white cat seated themselves. The first dish was a pie made of young pigeons, and the next was a fricassee of the fattest mice. The view of the one made the prince almost afraid to taste the other; till the white cat, who guessed his thoughts, assured him that there were certain dishes at table in which there was not a morsel of either rat or mouse, which had been dressed on purpose for him: accordingly he ate heartily of such as she recommended.

When supper was over, the prince perceived that the white cat had a portrait set in gold hanging to one of her feet. He begged her permission to look at it; when, to his astonishment, he beheld the portrait of a handsome young man, who exactly resembled himself! He thought there was something very extraordinary in all this; yet, as the white cat sighed, and looked very sorrowful, he did not venture to ask any questions. He conversed with her on different subjects, and found her extremely well versed in everything that was passing in the world. When night was far advanced, the white cat wished him a good night, and he was conducted by the hands to his bedchamber, which was different still from anything he had seen in the palace, being hung with the wings of butterflies, mixed with the most curious feathers. His bed was of gauze, festooned with bunches of the gayest ribbons, and the looking glasses reached from the floor to the ceiling. The prince was undressed and put to bed by the hands without speaking a word: he, however, slept little, and in the morning was awaked by a confused noise. The hands took him out of bed, and put on him a handsome hunting jacket. He looked into the courtyard, and perceived more than five hundred cats busily employed in preparing for the field; for this was a day of festival. Presently the white cat came to his apartment, and, having politely inquired after his health, she invited him to partake of their amusement. The prince willingly accepted her invitation, and mounted a wooden horse, richly caparisoned, which had been prepared for him, and which he was assured would gallop to admiration. The beautiful white cat mounted a monkey, dressed in a dragon bonnet, which made her look so fierce that all the rats and mice ran away in the utmost terror.

Everything being ready, the horns sounded, and away they went. No hunting was ever more agreeable; the cats ran faster than the hares and rabbits, and, when they caught any, they were hunted in the presence of the white cat, and a thousand cunning tricks were played. Nor were birds in safety; for the monkey made nothing of climbing up the trees, with the white cat on his back, to the nest of the young eagles. When the hunting was over, the whole retinue returned to the palace; and the white cat immediately exchanged her dragon cap for the veil, and sat down to supper with the prince, who, being very hungry, ate heartily, and afterwards partook of the most delicious liqueurs—which being often repeated, made him forget that he was to procure a little dog for the old king. He thought no longer of anything but of pleasing the sweet little creature who received him so courteously; accordingly, every day was passed in new amusements.

The prince had almost forgotten his country and relations, and sometimes even regretted that he was not a cat, so great was his affection for his mewing companions. " Alas! " said he to the white cat, " how will it afflict me to leave you whom I love so much! Either make yourself a lady, or make me a cat." She smiled at the prince's wish, but made him scarcely any reply. At length the twelvemonth was nearly expired: the white cat, who knew the very day when the prince was to reach his father's palace, reminded him that he had but three days longer to look for a perfect little dog. The prince, astonished at his own forgetfulness, began to afflict himself; when the cat told him not to be so sorrowful, since she would not only provide him with a little dog, but also with a wooden horse, which should convey him safely in less than twelve hours. " Look here," said she, showing him an acorn; " this contains what you desire." The prince put the acorn to his ear, and heard the barking of a little dog. Transported with joy, he thanked the cat a thousand times; and the next day, bidding her tenderly adieu, he set out on his return.

The prince arrived first at the place of rendezvous, and was soon joined by his brothers. They mutually embraced, and began to give an account of their success; when the youngest showed them only a little mongrel cur, telling them he thought it could not fail to please the king, from its extraordinary beauty. The brothers trod on each other's toes under the table, as much as to say, "We have little to fear from this sorry-looking animal." The next day they went together to the palace. The dogs of the two elder brothers were lying on cushions, and so curiously wrapped around with embroidered quilts that one would scarcely venture to touch them. The youngest produced his cur, dirty all over, and all wondered how the prince could hope to receive a crown for such a present. The king examined the two little dogs of the elder princes, and declared he thought them so equally beautiful that he knew not to which, with justice, he could give the preference. They accordingly began to dispute: when the youngest prince, taking his acorn from his pocket, soon ended their contention; for a little dog appeared, which could with ease go through the smallest ring, and was, besides, a miracle of beauty. The king could not possibly hesitate in declaring his satisfaction: yet, as he was not more inclined than the year before to part with his crown, he could think of nothing more to his purpose than telling his sons that he was extremely obliged to them for the pains they had taken; and, since they had succeeded so well, he could not but wish they would make a second attempt. He therefore begged they would take another year for procuring him a piece of cambric, so fine as to be drawn through the eye of a small needle.

The three princes thought this very hard, yet they set out in obedience to the king's command. The two eldest took different roads: and the youngest remounted his wooden horse, and in a short time arrived at the palace of his beloved white cat, who received him with the greatest joy, while the trunkless hands helped him to dismount and provided him with immediate refreshments; after which the prince gave the white cat an account of the admiration which had been bestowed on the beautiful little dog, and informed her of the further injunction of his father. "Make yourself perfectly easy, my dear prince," said she. "I have in my palace some cats that are perfectly clever in making such cambric as the king requires; so you have nothing to do but to give me the pleasure of your company while it is making, and I will procure you all the amusement possible." She accordingly ordered the most curious fire-works to be played off in sight of the window of the apartment in which they were sitting, and nothing but festivity and rejoicing were heard throughout the palace for the prince's return.

As the white cat frequently gave proofs of an excellent under-standing, the prince was by no means tired of her company. She talked with him of state affairs, of theatres, of fashions—in short, she was at a loss on no subject whatever; so that, when the prince was alone, he had plenty of amusement in thinking how it could possibly be that a small white cat could be endowed with all the powers of human creatures.

The twelvemonth in this manner again passed insensibly away, but the cat took care to remind the prince of his duty in proper time. "For once, my prince," said she, "I will have the pleasure of equipping you as suits your high rank:" when, looking into the courtyard, he saw a superb car, ornamented all over with gold, silver, pearls, and diamonds, drawn by twelve horses as white as snow, and harnessed in the most sumptuous trappings; and behind the car, a thousand guards, richly apparelled, were in waiting to attend on the prince's person. She then presented him with a nut: "you will find in it," said she, "the piece of cambric I promised you; do not break the shell till you are in the presence of the king your father." Then, to prevent the acknowledgments which the prince was about to offer, she hastily bade him adieu.

Nothing could exceed the speed with which the snow-white horses conveyed this fortunate prince to his father's palace, where his brothers had just arrived before him. They embraced each other, and demanded an immediate audience of the king, who received them with the greatest kindness. The princes hastened to place at the feet of his majesty the curious present he had required them to procure. The eldest produced a piece of cambric that was so extremely fine that his friends had no doubt of its passing the eye of the needle, which was now delivered to the king, having been kept locked up in the custody of his majesty's treasurer all the time. Everyone supposed he would certainly obtain the crown; but when the king tried to draw it through the eye of the needle, it would not pass, though it failed but very little. Then came the second prince, who made as sure of obtaining the crown as his brother had done; but, alas! with no better success; for though the piece of cambric was exquisitely fine, yet it could not be drawn through the eye of the needle.

It was now the youngest prince's turn; who accordingly advanced, and, opening an elegant little box inlaid with jewels, he took out a walnut and cracked the shell, imagining he should immediately perceive his piece of cambric; but what was his astonishment, to see nothing but a filbert! He did not, however, lose his hopes; he cracked the filbert, and it presented him with a cherry stone. The lords of the court, who had assembled to witness this extraordinary trial, could not, any more than the princes his brothers, refrain from laughing, to think he should be so silly as to claim with them the crown on no better pretensions. The prince, however, cracked the cherry stone, which was filled with a kernel: he divided it, and found in the middle a grain of wheat, and in that a grain of millet seed. He was now absolutely confounded, and could not help muttering between his teeth, "O white cat! white cat! thou hast deceived me!" At this moment he felt his hand scratched by the claw of a cat, upon which he again took courage; and, opening the grain of millet seed, to the astonishment of all present he drew forth a piece of cambric four hundred yards long, and fine enough to be drawn with perfect ease through the eye of the needle. When the king found he had no pretext for refusing the crown to his youngest son, he sighed deeply, and it was easy to be seen that he was sorry for the prince's success. " My sons," said he, " it is so gratifying to the heart of a father to receive proofs of his children's love, that I cannot refuse myself the satisfaction of requiring of you one thing more. You must undertake another expedition; and whichever by the end of the year brings me the most beautiful lady, shall marry her, and obtain my crown."

So they again took leave of the king and of each other, and set out without delay; and in less than twelve hours our young prince arrived in his splendid car at the palace of his dear white cat. Everything went on as before, till the end of another year. At length only one day remained of the year, when the white cat thus addressed him: "To-morrow, my prince, you must present yourself at the palace of your father, and give him a proof of your obedience. It depends only on yourself to conduct thither the most beautiful princess ever yet beheld; for the time is come when the enchantment by which I am bound may be ended. You must cut off my head and tail," continued she, "and throw them into the fire." "I?" said the prince, hastily; "I cut off your head and tail! You surely mean to try my affection, which, believe me, beautiful cat, is truly yours." "You mistake me, generous prince," said she. "I do not doubt your regard; but if you wish to see me in any other form than that of a cat, you must consent to do as I desire, when you will have done me a service I shall never be able sufficiently to repay." The prince's eyes filled with tears as she spoke, yet he considered himself obliged to undertake the dreadful task; and, the cat continuing to press him with greater eagerness, with a trembling hand he drew his sword, cut off her head and tail, and threw them into the fire.

No sooner was this done, than the most beautiful lady he had ever seen stood before him; and before he had sufficiently recovered from his surprise to speak to her, a long train of attendants, who at the same moment as their mistress were changed to their natural shapes, came to offer their congratulations to the queen, and inquire her commands. She received them with the greatest kindness, and ordering them to withdraw, thus addressed the astonished prince:—

"Do not imagine, dear prince, that I have always been a cat, or that I am of obscure birth. My father was the monarch of six kingdoms; he tenderly loved my mother, leaving her always at liberty to follow her own inclinations. Her prevailing passion was to travel; and a short time before my birth, having heard of some fairies who were in possession of the largest gardens, filled with the most delicious fruits, she had so strong a desire to eat some of them, that she set out for the country where they lived. She arrived at their abode, which she found to be a magnificent palace, on all sides glittering with gold and precious stones. She knocked a long time at the gates, but no one came, nor could she perceive the least sign that it had any inhabitant. The difficulty, however, did but increase the violence of my mother's longing; for she saw the tops of the trees above the garden walls, loaded with the most delicious fruits. The queen, in despair, ordered her attendants to place tents close to the door of the palace; but, having waited six weeks without seeing anyone pass the gates, she fell sick of vexation, and her life was despaired of.

"One night, as she lay half asleep, she turned herself about, and, opening her eyes, perceived a little old woman, very ugly and deformed, sitting in the easy chair by her bedside. 'I and my sister fairies,' said she, 'take it very ill that your majesty should so obstinately persist in getting some of our fruit; but since so precious a life is at stake, we consent to give you as much as you can carry away, provided you will give us in return what we shall ask.' 'Ah! kind fairy,' cried the queen, 'I will give you anything that I possess, even my very kingdoms, on condition that I eat of your fruit.' The old fairy then informed the queen that what they required was that she should give them the child she was going to have, as soon as she should be born; adding, that every possible care should be taken of her, and that she should become the most accomplished princess. The queen replied that, however cruel the condition, she must accept it, since nothing but the fruit could save her life. In short, dear prince,' continued the lady, 'my mother presently got out of bed, was dressed by her attendants, entered the palace, and satisfied her longing. When the queen had eaten her fill, she ordered four thousand mules to be provided, and loaded with the fruit, which had the virtue of continuing all the year round in a state of perfection.

" Thus provided, she returned to the king my father, who with the whole court received her with rejoicings, as it was before imagined she would die of disappointment. All this time the queen said nothing to my father of the promise she had made to give her daughter to the fairies; so that when the time was come that she expected my birth, she grew very melancholy; till at length, being pressed by the king, she declared to him the truth. Nothing could exceed his affliction, when he heard that his only child, when born, was to be given to the fairies. He bore it, however, as well as he could, for fear of adding to my mother's grief; and also believing he should find some means of keeping me in a place of safety, which the fairies would not be able to approach. As soon, therefore, as I was born, he had me conveyed to a tower in the palace to which there were twenty flights of stairs, and a door to each, of which my father kept the key; so that none came near me without his consent. When the fairies heard of what had been done, they sent first to demand me; and, on my father's refusal, they let loose a monstrous dragon, which devoured men, women, and children, and which, by the breath of its nostrils, destroyed everything it came near, so that the trees and plants began to die in great abundance. The grief of the king at seeing this could scarcely be equalled; and finding that his whole kingdom would in a short time be reduced to famine, he consented to give me into their hands.

"I was accordingly laid in a cradle of mother-of-pearl, ornamented with gold and jewels, and carried to their palace; when the dragon immediately disappeared. The fairies placed me in a tower of their palace, elegantly furnished, but to which there was no door, so that whoever approached was obliged to come by the windows, which were a great height from the ground; from these I had the liberty of getting out into a delightful garden, in which were baths and every sort of cooling fruit. In this place I was educated by the fairies, who behaved to me with the greatest kindness; my clothes were splendid, and I was instructed in every kind of accomplishment. In short, prince, if I had never seen anyone but themselves, I should have remained very happy. One of the windows of my tower overlooked a long avenue shaded with trees, so that I had never seen in it a human creature. One day, however, as I was talking at this window with my parrot, I perceived a young gentleman, who was listening to our conversation. As I had never seen a man but in pictures, I was not sorry for the opportunity of gratifying my curiosity. I thought him a very pleasing object, and he at length bowed in a most respectful manner, without daring to speak, for he knew that I was in the palace of the fairies. When it began to grow dark, he went away, and I vainly endeavoured to see which road he took. The next morning, as soon as it was light, I again placed myself at the window, and had the pleasure of seeing that the gentleman had returned to the same place. He now spoke to me through a speaking trumpet, and informed me he thought me a most charming lady; and that he should be very unhappy if he did not pass his life in my company.

"I resolved to find some means of escaping from my tower with the engaging prince I had seen. I was not long in devising the means for the execution of my project; I begged the fairies to bring me a netting needle, a mesh, and some cord, saying that I wished to make some nets, to amuse myself with catching birds at my window. This they readily complied with, and in a short time I completed a ladder long enough to reach the ground. I now sent my parrot to the prince to beg he would come to the usual place, as I wished to speak with him. He did not fail; and, finding the ladder, mounted it, and quickly entered my tower. This at first alarmed me; but the charms of his conversation had restored me to tranquillity, when all at once the window opened, and the Fairy Violent, mounted on the dragon's back, rushed into the tower. My beloved prince thought of nothing but how to defend me from their fury—for I had had time to relate to him my story, previous to this cruel interruption; but their numbers overpowered him, and the Fairy Violent had the barbarity to command the dragon to devour my prince before my eyes. In my despair, I would have thrown myself also into the mouth of the horrible monster; but this they took care to prevent, saying my life should be preserved for greater punishment. The fairy then touched me with her wand, and I instantly became a white cat. She next conducted me to this palace, which belonged to my father, and gave me a train of cats for my attendants, together with the twelve hands that waited on your highness. She then informed me of my birth, and the death of my parents; and pronounced upon me what she imagined the greatest of maledictions, that I should not be restored to my natural figure until a young prince, the perfect resemblance of him I had lost, should cut off my head and tail. You are that perfect resemblance; and accordingly, you ended the enchantment. I need not add, that I already love you more than my life; let us therefore hasten to the palace of the king your father, and obtain his approbation to our marriage."

The prince and princess accordingly set out side by side, in a car of still greater splendour than before, and reached the palace just as the two brothers had arrived with two beautiful princesses. The king, hearing that each of his sons had succeeded in finding what he had required, again began to think of some new expedient to delay the time of his resigning his crown; but when the whole court were with the king assembled to pass judgment, the princess who accompanied the youngest, perceiving his thoughts by his countenance, stepped majestically forward, and thus addressed him: " What pity, that your majesty, who is so capable of governing, should think of resigning the crown! I am fortunate enough to have six kingdoms in my possession: permit me to bestow one on each of the eldest princes, and to enjoy the remaining four in the society of the youngest. And may it please your majesty to keep your own kingdom, and make no decision concerning the beauty of the three princesses, who, without such proof of your majesty's preference, will no doubt live happily together." The air resounded with the applauses of the assembly; the young prince and princess embraced the king, and next their brothers and sisters; the three weddings immediately took place, and the kingdoms were divided as the princess had proposed.

Plantagenet.

PLANTAGENET.

In happy time and summer morning hour,
 I went, a gentle hermit for my guide,
Pleased to pursue the winding of the Stour
 Along the vale reflected in its tide:
 Where, seeking Cantuaria, beside
The mound of Chilham with its Roman crest,[1]
 Reluctantly the river seemed to glide—
 Slowly to leave the woodlands which invest
The precinct, linden-bowered, and fane of holy rest.

’Twas not for me that memories of dust
 Were in the venerable shade enshrined—
That marble virtues, weeping o’er their trust,[2]
 Around the monumental shaft reclined.
 The fretted tablet,[3] and the names which signed
Each gorgeous catacomb,[4] were read no more:
 Mine was the freedom of a careless mind,
 Musing, and weaving on the fertile shore
Its own imaginings—a bright and countless store.

Albeit the sacred portal might enclose
 A twicetold record of untimely fate—[5]
A father’s, honoured in his last repose.[6]
 What duteous forms upon his impress wait!

Chantrey ! 'twas thine alone to animate
That matron brow, beneath her hand compressed,
  In tears—that kneeling sorrow to create,
With hidden face, whose foot escapes her vest—
The manly filial grief in pious looks expressed.

  Not, then, for me—the valley was mine own.
    My senses with the morning air inhaled
Incense and health : each early sound well known—
    Bird-note, and hum of insect tribes—prevailed.
    In azure deepening the thin cloud sailed,
Tipped at each interstice with orient light;
    Then, as the golden sun arose, unveiled,
Remoter beauties grew upon the sight—
Streamlet, and fold, and wood, and range of verdant height.

  Should not the heart awaken with the ray,
    Chastened in all but grateful humble glow?
For refuge past and present bounty pay
    Its solemn thanksgiving, and frame the vow
    (So Heaven, in its mercy, should bestow
Purpose of holiness and help benign),
    To win another day of price below;
Waiting the morn that shall for ever shine,
The beatific change from mortal to divine?

  But this was pleasant day of little task,
    Redeemed from graver offices profound,
To meet a friend's society—to ask
    His guidance over his paternal ground,
    And broader fields which circle it around.
The lordly herd reposed upon the plain
    Of Eastwell, with its beechen thicket crowned;
Each maze extended to the pilgrim twain,
And in the horizon slept the distant silver main.

The graceful trees, in many a long arcade,
    Smooth-stemmed and bright, diverged upón the wold,
And yet the silence and the untroubled shade
    Of human intervention little told.
    Where'er the trunk was rooted from its hold,
Its lord allowed it picturesque decay,
    With all its leafy honours ; and behold,
Apart, the red stag keep his lonely sway,
And eye the approaching wight with dull yet fierce survey.

The wood-path ceased behind us, and our march
    Declined upon the herd-bespotted green,
The white extending walls and portal arch
    Of distant Eastwell in the bright serene.
    Not yet the awaiting steed and train were seen,
Nor cavalier with beauty by his side.
    We wandered on amid the varied scene,
A nameless rivulet alone our guide,
Pouring among the sedge its undiscovered tide.

We lingered underneath a lonely thorn,
    With venerable trunk of mossy grey
And root by clustering of cattle worn,
    To listen to the water on its way
    Along a copse of elm and alder spray
And verdant sedges bright with many a flower.
    The village company, on Sabbath-day,
Might gather churchward by the spreading bower,
And over it arose their ancient holy tower.

And this is lowly restingplace of thine,
    Without a title on thy nameless stone,
Last-blooming scion of a regal line ! [7]
    Far happier, among these fields, unknown

(Health, and content, and industry thine own),
　　To fill thy course of unambitious years,
　　　Than occupy—sad heritage! a throne,
　With all a monarch's lot of cares and fears.
Then sink in hallowed rest among thy rude compeers!

But, must the glorious ensign of thy race,
　　The plant of emerald bedropped with gold,
　Be lost for ever from heroic place—
　　The beauteous brow, and helmet of the bold?
　　Shall princely standard never more unfold
The roses twain which lily flowers entwine;
　　Nor chivalry receive, nor valour hold
His azure circlet and his knighthood's sign
From honour-giving hand of any of thy line? [8]

Yet will not one, in after years, forget,
　　Who blushes as he tunes his humble song,
That memory of lost Plantagenet
　　Does to his modest lineage belong.
　　Not vaunting he the crown, nor sceptered throng,
Nor proud career of rivalry and fame;
　　But that the lovely loveliest among
Was she by whom his vain pretension came— [9]
Untimely lost on earth, in heaven a written name.

And, if the solitary voice were true
　　That lulled to motherless repose her son—
Of all the loveliest the world e'er knew,
　　Was loved more dearly, so lamented, none.
　　Not, if I trusted to the father tone
That taught an iteration of her name
　　To one instructed in its sound alone,
Ere, with the mind's new consciousness, came
The thought affectionate which hallowed that acclaim,

Receiving power with time; most powerful still
    In moments when that tender voice impressed
Its sweet communion; aiding thus to fill
    His own paternal admonitions best.
    And when his faithful spirit sank to rest,
Her lovéd idea, long and last retained,
    Amid the vital throbbings of his breast,
Unconquerable in its fervour reigned,
With life alone resigned. How soon to be regained!

Now, strike the chord! the poesy adorn!
    O prince! an echo from thy nameless shrine
Repeats the salutation of the morn,
    Accepting this untutored strain of mine;
    Not such as sounded in the martial line
Of him, the first Plantagenet, who spread [10]
    Upon Hibernian breeze his leopard sign—
Not such as wailed when gouts of crimson, shed [11]
For his repentant son, bedewed the kingly dead.

Hark to the cornet and the dulcimer,
    Immingling Moslem notes, in Syrian land,
With merry England's music! who, for her,
    Waves over humbled Saladin his hand?
    Heart of the lion, he! The breeze which fanned
His conquest, favours not the tempest-tossed.
    O seek him captive, thou, of all his band [12]
Of knightly troubadours regarded most!
Ye song-beleaguered walls! resign, resign the lost.

But there is memory of fairer bloom
    Than victor laurel, or the wreath of power,
For him who paid the author of his doom [13]
    With gifts of forfeit life and kingly dower.

The rose of chivalry may shed its flower;
　The monarch, in his blood-stained triumph, sigh;
　　But mercy visits earth as sweetest shower— 14
　Its odour reascends, as dew, on high,
Or aspiration pure when seraph aid is nigh.

Hail, freedom's charter, yielded to our sires!
　Hail, long and bloodless rule of Henry's day!
Amid the awakening of glory's fires,
　Ye passed not unrevered and lost away;
　And e'en the lustre of that holy ray
Which shed itself on Salem's lost alcove,
　Lives not in legends old and minstrel lay
Like hers, of matchless constancy, above 15
All other matron names in her devoted love.

Veil his pavilion from the sultry wind,
　And bid the service of his minions cease!
The prince, unarmed, and on his couch reclined,
　Has ear for one alone who speaks of peace.
　The flowing vestments from their fold release,
Amid that conference, the suitor's hand;
　And, while he feigns solicitude to piece
His Paynim speech with Norman phrases bland,
He strikes at Edward's side with death-devoting brand.

Then woke the lion spirit! then, the strength 16
　Of all the kings and heroes of his line!
His foot has laid the recreant at length,
　While yet in act to master his design.
　Those giant arms in their embraces twine
The prostrate, and usurp his conquered steel,
　Which issues of his heart incarnadine;
And those who gather, at their lord's appeal,
Come but to spurn the corse in their officious zeal.

And has the treason impotently sped?
   The poniard, as he turned its point away,
Left on his arm its impress, sanguine red.
   O slight memorial of foul affray,
   Had poison not imbued it! skilful they
By whom the rankling sore is lanced and bound;
   But still the subtle venom holds its sway,
And, failing help, he dies! that help is found
On Eleanora's lips, which suck the throbbing wound.

Most fortunate in thy devotedness [17]
   Of honourable women! I have strayed [18]
Along the vales which Ley and Avon bless,
   By holy crosses, where thy corse was stayed,
   Ere, at thine end of honoured days, they laid
The queenly relic in Saint Peter's shrine;
   And heard, at evening, youth and village maid
Tell of thy faithful love in Palestine,
And bless, for thee, Castile, proud native land of thine.

I too have wandered, with averted eyes,
   Amid the fields where Severn flows unseen; [19]
And sped, in fantasy, to other skies,
   Of retribution, not of crime, the scene. [20]
   O miserable days, and few, between
The murderous vigil and the midnight snare
   Which held the partner of a guilty queen!
O filial revenge! too fierce to " spare
The gentle Mortimer," at Isabella's prayer!

Mount high, Plantagenet! thy ruling star,
   Ascendant, holds its influences bright
O'er ocean, rolling with the tide of war— [21]
   O'er Picardy, the triple-banded height, [22]

Whence England's lord, unaiding, views the fight,
   And speeds but to salute his victor son—
   O'er Thames, re-echoing with proud delight,
   Where, humble and serene, is he, alone,[23]
Who brings a captive king before his father's throne.

The fallen scarf [24]—the blush, exchanged for pride,
   Of her who moved from Windsor's courtly maze,
   A royal moralist to grace her side,
   And bid the chivalry adopt his phrase—
   These are the lighter honours of the days.
More high, alas! the sorrow, mute and dread,[25]
   Wherewith a mourning nation early lays
In Austin's sepulchre the mighty dead,
And with her sable prince laments her genius fled.

The heroic fail, the virtuous decline,
   Their auspices desert the fortunate.
Alas! and shall misdeeming man repine,
   Unhappy Richard! at thy nameless fate?[26]
   Thy footsteps pass no more the prison gate,
And numbered days of penance are thine own;
   Yet envy not high Lancaster the weight
Of hidden grief he clutches with the crown— [27]
His languor for content, from royal pillow flown.

For France! for France! the breeze, as it propels
   A hostile navy through the curling spray,
Is less aspiring than the hope that swells,
   Those gallant hearts which scorn the wind's delay.
   Soon, Harfleur's lords, and bound to Calais, they.[28]
The pass of interwinding Somme is short;
   But famine and disease obstruct the way;
And such the captives France has sold and bought,[29]
For ransoms to be earned in battle yet unfought.

The milkwhite courser and resplendent mail [30]
 Are his who may disturb a dream so bright:
His enterprise, his fortitude, prevail.
 Whether, with hope redeemed from thickest fight,
 His three companions each in death a knight [31]
He signs at Agincourt—or, crowned and stoled,[32]
 He sits, fair Paris! at thy festal rite—
Or hears by weeping friend his summons told—[33]
Of kingly men the first, and bravest of the bold.

And thou, meek offspring of a puissant sire!
 Ill-fortuned father of a princely·son! [34]
Yet shall not youth and lettered age retire
 By early Thames, and Cam, slow-gliding on,
 Who name thee not in grateful orison
Beneath the cloisters it was thine to raise.[35]
 Alas for England, doubly lost and won,
Unworthy to divide with thee the praise!
Alas, that rule of thine was cast in evil days!

The parted scions of the royal tree [36]
 Bequeathed alike a long descending claim
Of sad inheritance, most sad to thee!
 Witness the fold and hearth enwrapped in flame;
 The kindred slaughter: and to him who came
To ask thy crown—alas, a fatal quest! [37]
 Among the rival offspring of his name
A portion brief of triumph ill possessed—
Unsparing of their own,[38] and Bosworth field for rest!

But he, who sleeps at Eastwell,[39] mingled not
 Among the high pretenders of the day.
A tranquil dawn of privacy his lot,
 And gentle nurture—not parental, they

Who ruled; but it was pleasant to obey.
Once only, summoned to a brighter scene,
   He trode with them such chamber of array
As Barnard's or as Crosby Hall have been,[40]
And bowed his knee to one of grave and lofty mien.

The princely looks, on which attention hung,
   To him with fond complacency inclined—
Caressing hands around his forehead clung,
   And in the clusters of his hair were twined;
   And this the counsel graven on his mind—
" Pursue, fair boy! such exercise as leads
   To knightly honour, and be sure to find
A friend who will not fail thee.   What succeeds
Is in award of Heaven, which prospers gallant deeds."

Forth from the presence and its state retired
   The stripling, rapt in visions bright and fair;
His youthful heart with emulation fired,
   And all that monitor enjoined his care.
   Soon was his practice mastery; and where
The friend who pledged him to such high emprise?
   Some few short months, and royal pages bare
A mandate which, in his delighted eyes,
Bore augury of bright and famous destinies.

Upon his cheek his manhood's primal down,
   O'er all his looks ingenuous joy was spread;
And never fairer suitor to renown
   Essayed to win her, wheresoe'er she led.
   A moment, and his farewell smile was shed
On home and cherished friends, and he was gone:
   Of each retiring steed his own the head,
His eye responsive to the bugle tone,
And all he saw surpassing fair—to him alone.

Around were none without a mien to grace
   The courtly hall and retinue of kings,
Or hold in chivalry a gentle place;
   But each, amid his own imaginings,
   Which haply dwelt on grave and doubtful things,
Found little parley to beguile the way,
   Such as a cheerful mind to converse brings;
Yet in observance prompt, and courteous, they,
Until their ready speed had worn an autumn day.

"And what the stream which peacefully among
   The twilight harvest wanders, cool and clear?
The towers and battlements, to which belong
   Yon lines of scattered township in their rear?"
   " The limpid Soar, and Leicester guild, are near.
'Tis ours to find the king, at his behest;
   Soon will his royal armament appear,
Encamped to-night on Bosworth's heathy breast.
Pursue your speed, fair sir! the light deserts the west."

The star of eve no more was eminent,
   And heavy clouds obscured the northern wain,
Before the liegemen at the royal tent
   Resigned their charge to an attendant train.
   Then was an interval for thought.   How vain!
The tramp of horse, the password and reply,
   The din of arms, resounded o'er the plain.
He cast across the tent an eager eye:
Its curtain was withdrawn, and hasty steps drew nigh.

The foremost of a noble escort came—
   Once, doubtfully, more fitly homaged, now:
His presence and commanding port the same,
   But where his graver look and thoughtful brow?

Relinquished for the keen and thrilling glow
Of confidence in arms.   A moment's space
    He gazed upon young Richard, kneeling low;
Motioned his followers from their meetingplace,
And raised and clasped the youth in unrestrained embrace.

    " Our son "—the name he uttered was no less—
    " Between us lives, alas! no longer one; [41]
And, with the morrow's well assured success,
    England shall find thee near our royal throne.
    This seal and high commission are thine own—[42]
They give thee Calais, Guisnes, with our domain
    In France; and better shall our love be shown,
When foul rebellion has discharged this stain,
And loyalty unblamed may lift his head again."

    His lofty tone was for a moment lowered;
    A flash of dark expression in his eye,
Which warily upon his hearer cowered :
    While, thus—" To-morrow we must reign, or die.
    Our will recoils not from a gage so high,
Befitting well the kingborn and the brave.
    Thou, should our battle be successless, fly,
For hour more fortunate; thy sire will have,
At least, a brave revenge, a royal soldier's grave."

He spoke, and added from his treasure store
    Of gold and gems, a rich inheritance,
Heaped with parental bounty; and no more
    He signed, howe'er indulgent of the glance
    Which passed the dower and rested on the lance.
" Thou shalt have chivalry in happy tide."
    Then, " Hark! our angry clarions sound advance.
Retire a space, with Radcliff for thy guide, [43]
And stand in future fields at victor Richard's side."

The land had rest, and memories were few
   Of royal Henry's battle for his crown.
Before the Lord of Eastwell smiled in view
   His pleasant fields and his romantic down,
   The browsing herds, and green sward newly mown.
He walked, and visited the rural care
   Of hind and herdsman; and, in cheerful tone,
Gave and returned a patriarchal prayer,[44]
Like him of Bethlehem—like him a blessing bare.

'Twas not the labour of the field alone
   That tasked his willing peasantry; they hewed
The beam prepared, or smoothed the massive stone.
   Unwonted service for the wild and rude!
   And, but that one with better skill endued,
A gentle stranger, lent his timely aid,
   Eastwell had long been rural solitude—
A lovely wilderness of down and glade,
Nor hospitable roof nor genial hearth arrayed.

The patron, as, at intervals, he found
   That stranger from the task he ceased to guide
Retired apart, and fixed in thought profound,
   Would pause awhile, and parley at his side.
   Such answers as the listener supplied
Were formed in plain and unassuming phrase,
   Befitted to the part he occupied.
'Twas long before the practised ear and gaze
Had deemed of him as one declined from better days.

He chanced, at summer eventime, to stray
   Beneath the wood, his occupation o'er—
Unwitting that the knight had sought the way—
   And contemplated tome of ancient lore.

His patron marked the characters it bore :
To read had puzzled a more clerkly man.
  And, with the thoughts he had repressed before,
  A glow of higher sympathy began.
The secret was inquired, and told, and thus it ran.

" The lot which placed the crown on Henry's brow,
  Cost me a royal father.   Men may blame
King Richard ; it becomes his son to know
  That well he merited his valour's fame :[45]
  And once, at least, might pity hail his name,
Who spared Lord Stanley's blood, his own the cost. [46]
  Mine was, alas ! redeemed for flight and shame
Among the scattered relics of his host,
Attainted from the hour when he was found and lost.

His very bounty, meeting vulgar eyes,
  Had moved suspicion fatal to this head.
I passed unheeded, in a low disguise,
  And question ceased of one accounted dead.
  The craft I chose, the simple life I led,
Accorded haply with my youthful prayer,
  Ere lost in visions which so darkly fled.
The time is past, and subterfuge my care
No further than for decency, which I would spare."[47]

The stranger ceased : his secret was a friend's
  As generous as noble.   Thus he said :
" Thy truant fortune owes thee some amends.
  The confidence I sought were ill repaid
  Without such counsel and protecting aid
As Eastwell's lord can offer.   Here abide.
  Thou'rt free to choose thy home within the glade ;
And, should affliction or mischance betide,
Seek then yon open door, and meet them at my side."

The happiest of Eastwell homes was one
　　Which reared its beechen-mantled roof between
The village churchway and the bench of stone
　　That served for council on the little green,
　　When toil was past and eventime serene.
The honeybee and martlet loved the spot;[48]
　　There rosemary and eglantine were seen;
The water welled beneath the simplest grot;
And children went to play and linger round the cot.

There, dispossessing nature's occupants,
　　The friend unknown of Moyle had built a cell,
Sufficient for the few and simple wants
　　Of one who as an anchorite could dwell.
　　But when was hermitage purveyed so well?
His missal was not all his learned store.
　　The villagers with whom he came to dwell,
Their benefactor, friend, and playmate, bore
Their offerings unseen, and placed them at his door.

He, in his turn, had largess to bestow,
　　At festal times, the solemn and the gay,
On those who stood around in joyful row—
　　Himself less loud, but as serene as they.
　　He was the mansion's guest, on holiday,
Welcomed and cherished.　Such the life he led;
　　Thus its continued seasons passed away;
And years which gathered on his hoary head
Were calm and blissful all, until fourscore had sped.[49]

Who learned at Eastwell, or who heeded there,
　　That, twice, a Tudor had demised the throne,
And that the latest Henry's youthful heir
　　Looked from an earthly toward a saintly one?

'Twas then the pilgrim's numbered days were gone.
Silent, except in prayer and praise, he lay,
   With many friends around ; but only known
To one who, when his spirit passed away,
Was there to close his eyes, and wrap his lifeless clay.

He died unnamed ; and then his friends were told
   That he, whose sun thus peacefully had set—
Whom, weeping, they had laid in hallowed mould—
   Was, by his filial right, Plantagenet.
   The chronicle alone survives him yet :
The tomb, accounted his, has lost its shield,[50]
   And stands without a title ; men forget [51]
His place, unnoted in the verdant field ;
The little gushing well, that gave him drink, is sealed.

But not, like them, are transient and fleet
   The moral power and beauty of the tale.
The memory of pious worth is sweet,
   When things material and mortal fail :
   Admonishing that faith and hope prevail
In pure and humble minds, and only those,
   When trials and solicitudes assail ;
And that afflictions of the good disclose
Their latent virtue best, and bring them to repose.

NOTES.

¹ *The mound of Chilham, with its Roman crest.*

Chilham, not far from the river Stour, is supposed to have been the place where Julius Cæsar encamped, in his second expedition to Britain; and that from hence it was at first called Julham—*i. e.,* Julius's house: and below the town there is a green barrow called Jul-laber, which is thought to be the grave of Laberius Dorus, the tribune, who was killed by the Britons in the march of the Romans from that camp. Afterwards it came to be the seat of the kings of Kent, and it had a castle. It was transferred by marriage, in 1636, to Sir Dudley Digges, Master of the Rolls, who erected a noble building on the ruins of the castle. Chilham Castle is now the property of James B. Wildman, Esq.

² *That marble virtues, weeping o'er their trust,*
Around the monumental shaft reclined.

In a chapel, on the south side of the chancel at Chilham, is an alabaster column, having its pedestal supported by statues representing the four cardinal virtues; erected in 1638, by Sir Dudley Digges, to the memory of his lady.

³ *The fretted tablet.*

A stately monument in the north transept of Chilham Church, with a laudatory inscription, in honour of Margaret, sister of Sir Dudley Digges, and wife of Sir Anthony Palmer, deceased 1619, in the thirty-third year of her age.

⁴ *The names which signed*
Each gorgeous catacomb.

The catacombs surround the magnificent circular mausoleum of the Colebroke family, sometime possessors of Chilham Castle, on the north of the chancel.

⁵ *A twicetold record of untimely fate.*

At the south-west corner of Chilham Church are two monuments, each commemorating three children of Samuel and Mary Sherson Dick—namely,

Caroline Oakley Dick, born 1817, died 1831.
Robert Mantell Dick, „ 1814, „ 1832, Feb.
Samuel William Dick, „ 1813, „ 1832, Dec.

⁶ *A father's, honoured in his last repose.*

Mr. Wildman has erected on the north side of the chancel of Chilham Church, to the memory of his father, James Wildman, Esq., deceased in 1816, a beautiful monument by Chantrey, representing a sarcophagus, impressed with a medallion of Mr. Wildman, and surrounded by the figures of a matron, maiden, and youth, each finely expressive of reverential sorrow.

⁷ *Last-blooming scion of a regal line.*

" Wye Hundred, Eastwell :—There is a tradition that a natural son of King Richard the Third, named Richard Plantagenet, fled hither from Leicester, immediately after the fatal battle of Bosworth, fought in 1485, in which the king lost both his life and crown; and that he lived here in a mean capacity, having leave given him by Sir Thomas Moyle, so soon as he was discovered by him, to build for himself a small house in one of his fields, near his mansion of Eastwell Place, in which he afterwards lived and died: which is corroborated by an entry of his burial in the parish registry."

HASTED'S KENT.

⁸ *From honour-giving hand of any of thy line.*

" A soldier, by the honour-giving hand
Of Cœur-de-Lion knighted on the field."

SHAKSPEARE (K. John).

⁹ *She by whom his vain pretension came.*

Sophia, fifth daughter of the Rev. Jeremy Pemberton, of Trumpington House, Cambridgeshire, and maternally descended from Anne Plantagenet, sister of King Edward the Fourth—married to the Rev. Thomas Ripley.

¹⁰ *The first Plantagenet, who spread*
Upon Hibernian breeze his leopard sign.

The conquest of Ireland was made in the year 1171, by Henry the Second, the first King of England of the Plantagenet race, who obtained a grant of the island from Pope Adrian the Fourth.

¹¹ *When gouts of crimson, shed*
For his repentant son, bedewed the kingly dead.

" His corpse (that of King Henry the Second) was conveyed by his natural son Geoffry to the Nunnery of Fonterroult; and next day, while it lay in the abbey church, Richard, chancing to enter, was struck with horror at the sight. This, indeed, was augmented by an accident which the superstition of the times interpreted into a preternatural portent. At his approach, the blood gushed out of the mouth and nostrils of the corpse, to the horror and amazement of the spectators; and Richard's own savage heart was moved at this phenomenon. He assisted at the funeral rites with great decorum, and marks of real contrition."

SMOLLETT.

[12] *O seek him captive, thou, of all his band*
Of knightly troubadours regarded most!
Ye song-beleaguered walls! resign, resign the lost.

"The Englishmen were more than a whole yeare without hearing any tidings of their king, or in what place he was kept prisoner. He had trained up in his court a rimer or minstrill, called Blondell de Nesle, who (so saith the manuscript of old poesies, and an auncient manuscript French chronicle), being so long without the sight of his lord, his life seemed wearisome to him, and he became confounded with melancholly. Known it was that he came back from the Holy Land, but none could tell in what country he arrived. Whereupon, this Blondell, resolving to make search for him in many countries, but he would heare some news of him, after expence of divers dayes in travell he came to a towne (by good hap) near to the castell where his master King Richard was kept. Of his host he demanded to whom the castell appertained, and the host told him that it belonged to the Duke of Austria. Then he enquired whether there were any prisoners therein detained, or no; for always he made such secret questionings, wheresoever he came: and the host gave answer that there was one only prisoner, but he knew not what he was, and yet he had been detained there more then the space of a yeare. When Biondell heard this, he wrought such meanes that he became acquainted with them of the castell, as minstrills doe easily win acquaintance, any where; but to see the king he could not, neither understand that it was he. One day he sat directly before a window of the castell where King Richard was kept prisoner, and began to sing a song in French which King Richard and Blondell had sometime composed together. When King Richard heard the song, he knew it was Blondell that sung it; and when Blondell paused at the half of the song, the king began the other half, and completed it. Thus Blondell won the knowledge of the king his master, and, returning home into England, made the barons of the countrie acquainted where the king was."

From MONS. FAVINE. *See* PERCY'S "ESSAY
ON THE ANCIENT MINSTRELS."

K

[13] *Who paid the author of his doom*
With gifts of forfeit life and kingly dower.

" The Castle of Chalus being taken, he ordered Bertram de
Gourdon, who had shot the arrow, to be brought into his presence,
and asked what injury he had done him, that he should take away
his life. The other answered, with great deliberation, that he had
with his own hand slain his father and two brothers; and that he
should suffer cheerfully all the torments which could be inflicted,
since he had been the instrument of Providence that had delivered
the world of such a tyrant, who had filled it with blood and carnage.
Richard, struck with this answer, ordered the soldier to be presented
with one hundred shillings and set at liberty."

SMOLLETT.

Mercy visits earth as sweetest shower.

" It droppeth, as the gentle rain from heaven
Upon the place beneath."

SHAKSPEARE (Merchant of Venice).

[15] *Above*
All other matron names in her devoted love.

" Though the old man of the mountain had been taken in his
capital by the Tartars, and put to the sword with all his followers
who were found in the place, there still remained an assassin who
had been educated under him, and undertook to murder the prince
of England.

" This ruffian was furnished with letters from the Governor of
Joppa, proposing a negotiation; and, by virtue of these, obtained
admittance to Edward, who conversed with him freely, at different
times, in the French language, which the infidel understood. Hav-
ing thus secured free egress and regress, he entered the prince's
apartment on the Friday in Whitsun Week, and, the weather being
extremely sultry, found him sitting on his bed, in a loose garment.
There was no other person in the room but the assassin, who,
thinking this a proper opportunity to perpetrate his design, snatched
a dagger from his bosom, and attempted to plunge it into the prince's
belly. Edward, endeavouring to parry the stroke, received a deep
wound in his arm; and, perceiving the infidel about to repeat his
blow, struck him with his foot on the breast so forcibly that he fell
upon the ground: then, wresting the weapon from his hand, buried
it instantly in his heart.

" The domestics, hearing a noise, broke into the room; and one
of them, transported with rage and apprehension, snatched up a
joint stool, with which he dashed out the brains of the dead assassin.

The wound which Edward had received was the more dangerous as having been inflicted with a poisoned dagger; and the flesh beginning to exhibit signs of a gangrene, he made his will, and resigned himself to his fate : but, by the extraordinary skill of an English surgeon, the mortified parts were scarified, and the cure completed in little more than a fortnight."

SMOLLETT.

16 *The strength
Of all the kings and heroes of his line.*

" Yesterday, and the day before, you have condemned loyal and honourable blood to be poured forth like water: spare not mine. Were that of all my ancestors in my veins, I would have perilled it in this quarrel."

WAVERLEY: McIvor.

17 *Most fortunate in thy devotedness
Of honourable women!*

" She was daughter of Ferdinand, King of Castile, and married to Edward the First, King of England, with whom she went into the Holy Land. When her husband was treacherously wounded by a Moor, with a poisoned sword, and rather grew worse than received any ease by what the physicians applied, she found out a remedy as new and unheard of, as full of love and endearment. For, by reason of the malignity of the poison, her husband's wounds could not possibly be closed; but she licked them daily with her own tongue, and sucked out the venomous humour, thinking it a most delicious liquor: by the power whereof, or rather, by the virtue of a wife's tenderness, she so drew out the poisonous matter that he was entirely cured of his wound, and she escaped without catching any harm."

CAMDEN'S BRITANNIA.

18 *I have strayed
Along the vales which Ley and Avon bless;
By holy crosses, where thy corse was stayed.*

At Waltham West, on the river Ley, and near Northampton on the Avon (commonly called the New), are crosses, erected by King Edward the First in honour of Queen Eleanor—these being places where her corse rested in its way from Grantham in Lincolnshire, where she died, to Westminster Abbey.

19 *Amid the fields where Severn flows, unseen.*

Berkeley, where King Edward the Second was murdered, in the night of the 21st September, 1327.

K 2

[20] *Of retribution, not of crime, the scene.*

Nottingham, where Mortimer was surprised by the friends of King Edward the Third, who gained admittance to the castle by a subterranean passage leading from the cavern since called "Mortimer's hole," and made him prisoner.

"The queen, hearing the noise, and guessing the design of their coming, called aloud in the French language to her son, who she supposed to be at the head of the party, 'Fair son! fair son! have pity on the accomplished Mortimer.'"

SMOLLETT.

[21] *O'er ocean, rolling with the tide of war.*

The French fleet was totally defeated at Sluys by the English fleet, under the command of King Edward the Third in person, in the year 1340. Two of the French admirals, with upwards of twenty thousand men, and two hundred and thirty of their largest ships, were taken.

The Spanish fleet was defeated in 1350, also, by the king in person, off Winchelsea and Rye, where twenty-four large ships were taken.

[22] *O'er Picardy, the triple-banded height.*

Cressy, famous for the battle gained there by Edward the Third, against Philip the Sixth of France, in 1346.

"Those two lines (the English) were formed upon the declivity of the hill, in such a manner as to support one another. The king himself commanded the third line, posted on the brow of the eminence, behind the other two.

"The Earl of Warwick despatched a messenger to the king, desiring him to advance to the prince's succour. Edward, whom he found in a windmill, viewing the engagement, asked with great deliberation if his son was dead, wounded, or unhorsed; and, being answered in the negative, 'Well, then,' said he, 'go back and tell Warwick that I shall not intermeddle with the fray, but let my boy win his spurs by his own valour.'

"Edward, seeing the victory accomplished, descended from the hill, and, running up to the Prince of Wales, embraced him tenderly, in the sight of the whole army; saying, 'My valiant son, Heaven grant you may persevere in the course you have so gloriously begun! You have acquitted yourself nobly; and well are you worth the kingdom that will be your inheritance.' The prince made no other reply than that of a profound obeisance."

SMOLLETT.

23 *Where, humble and serene, is he, alone,*
     Who brings a captive king before his father's throne.

John, King of France, defeated and taken prisoner by Edward the Black Prince, in the battle of Poitiers, 1356.

" The royal prisoner. rode through the streets of London in a magnificent habit, mounted on a fine white courser, and attended by the Prince of Wales on a little black horse, with the ordinary trappings. The inhabitants vied with each other in displaying plate, tapestry, furniture, and arms offensive and defensive, in their shops, windows, and balconies. The streets were lined with an infinite concourse of people, and the cavalcade lasted from three in the morning till noon, when they reached Westminster Hall, where the King of England sat upon a royal throne, in expectation of their coming. He rose up when John approached, and received him with all that courteous civility which might be expected from a prince of his character. Then he embraced his son with great tenderness, and told him that the victory did not please him so much as the modesty with which he had borne his good fortune."

SMOLLETT.

24 *The fallen scarf.*

Tradition records that, the Countess of Shrewsbury having at a ball dropped her garter, King Edward the Third picked it up and presented it to her with the observation, " Honi soit qui mal y pense," which he caused to be adopted as a motto by the Knights of the Order of the Garter, which he instituted.

25 *More high, alas! the sorrow, mute and dread,*
     Wherewith a mourning nation early lays
     In Austin's sepulchre the mighty dead.

" Both Houses (of Parliament) attended the hearse of that beloved prince to Canterbury, where his obsequies were solemnized with great magnificence."

SMOLLETT.

26 *Unhappy Richard! at thy nameless fate.*

Richard the Second.

" The manner of his death is variously related. It seems more likely that he perished by famine; especially as the Archbishop of York, with the Earls of Northumberland and Worcester, when they afterwards revolted against Henry, affirmed in their manifesto that he was starved by being kept fifteen days without sustenance."

SMOLLETT.

[27] *His languor for content, from royal pillow flown.*

" As his constitution decayed, his fear of losing the crown re-
doubled, even to a childish anxiety. He would not sleep unless the
royal diadem was placed by his pillow."

SMOLLETT.

[28] *Soon, Harfleur's lords, and bound to Calais, they!*

" He (King Henry the Fifth) landed at the mouth of the Seine,
in Normandy, about three leagues from Harfleur, the siege of which
he undertook. The besieged, finding it impracticable to maintain
the place, capitulated.

"Finding it would be impracticable to winter at Harfleur, for
want of provision and forage, he, with the advice of his council,
resolved to begin his march by land for Calais, and to pass the
Somme at the place where it was forded by his great grandfather,
Edward the Third.

" His troops were afflicted with a dearth of provision, and total
want of necessaries—which, added to their distemper and the fatigues
they underwent, would have driven them to despair, had they not
been animated by the presence and example of their beloved
monarch, who shared in all their hardships, and encouraged them by
his alacrity."

SMOLLETT.

[29] *And such the captives France has sold and bought,*
   For ransoms to be earned in battle yet unfought.

" They (the French), when they considered the handful of English,
who did not exceed fourteen thousand enfeebled wretches, half dead
with famine and disease, looked upon the victory as having already
declared in their favour. They are even said to have played at dice
for the English prisoners before they were taken."

SMOLLETT.

[30] *The milkwhite courser and resplendent mail*
   Are his who may disturb a dream so bright.

" The king appeared in the front of the line, mounted on a stately
white charger, in splendid armour, with a golden crown fixed by
way of crest to his helmet: four royal banners were displayed before
him. He was followed by a great number of led horses in rich
caparisons, and surrounded by the chief officers of his court and
army."

SMOLLETT.

[31] *His three companions each in death a knight*
He signs at Agincourt.

" In all probability, he must have fallen a sacrifice to the determined resolution of these associates (eighteen French knights, who had determined to take him, dead or alive), had not David Gam, the Welsh captain, and two other officers of the same nation, rushed between him and the assailants, and lost their lives in his defence. When he recollected his spirits, he found these gallant soldiers dying of the wounds they had received, and knighted them as they lay upon the field of battle. The eighteen French knights were killed to a man."

SMOLLETT.

[32] *Or, crowned and stoled,*
He sits, fair Paris! at thy festal rite.

" On the day of Pentecost, 1422, the two kings and queens of France and England dined together in public, at Paris, with their crowns upon their heads."

SMOLLETT.

[33] *Or hears by weeping friend his summons told.*

" He inquired of his physicians how long they thought he should live; when one of them, kneeling by the bedside, while the tears trickled down his cheeks, declared that, without a miracle, two hours would put an end to his life. He heard this dreadful sentence without the least emotion."

SMOLLETT.

[34] *Ill-fortuned father of a princely son!*

" The Prince of Wales, falling into the hands of his enemies, was brought into the presence of Edward, who, with an air of insolence, demanded how he durst presume to enter his kingdom in arms? To this arrogant question he replied, with great fortitude and dignity, that he had come to recover his father's crown and his own inheritance, which Edward had unjustly usurped."

SMOLLETT.

[35] *Beneath the cloisters it was thine to raise.*

" He (Henry the Sixth) founded the College of Eton, near Windsor; and King's College, in Cambridge, for the reception of those scholars who had begun their studies at Eton."

[36] *The parted scions of the royal tree.*

John of Gaunt, Duke of Lancaster, fourth son of King Edward

the Third, and father of King Henry the Fourth; and Lionel, Duke
of Clarence, third son of King Edward the Third, and ancestor of
Richard, Duke of York, father of King Edward the Fourth.

[37] *And to him, who came*
To ask thy throne—alas! a fatal guest.

The Duke of York was slain, fighting on foot, at the battle of
Wakefield, in Yorkshire, against the royal forces, 1460.

[38] *Unsparing of their own.*

The Duke of Clarence was put to death by his brother, King
Edward the Fourth; and Edward the Fifth dethroned by his uncle,
King Richard the Third.

[39] *He who sleeps at Eastwell.*

"On the north side of the chancel of Eastwell Church is an an-
cient tomb, which has been assigned to Richard Plantagenet, whom
a traditional tale represents as having been a natural son of Richard
the Third, and whose burial is thus recorded in the Register of East-
well, under the date 1550:—'✓ Rychard Plantagenet was buried the
22ʸ daye of Desember, anno ut supra.'* It is observable that a simi-
lar mark to that prefixed to the name of Plantagenet occurs before
every subsequent entry in the old Register where the person recorded
was of noble blood.

"The story of Richard Plantagenet has exercised the pen of
several writers; but the most particular account of his history, and
the most curious, was given in a letter from Dr. Thomas Brett, of
Spring Grove, in Wye Parish, to Dr. W. Warren—afterwards pub-
lished in Peck's 'Desiderata Curiosa,' from which the following
particulars are extracted:—

"'Now for the story of Richard Plantagenet. In the year 1720
(I have forgot the particular day, only remember it was about
Michaelmas) I waited on the late Lord Heneage, Earl of Winchelsea,
at Eastwell House, and found him sitting with the Register Book of
the Parish of Eastwell lying open before him. He told me he had
been looking there to see who of his own family were mentioned in
it. 'But,' says he, 'I have a curiosity here to show you;' and then
showed it me, and I immediately transcribed it into my almanack:—
'Rychard Plantagenet was buryed the 22 daye of Desember, anno
ut supra.' Ex registro de Eastwell, sub anno 1550.

"'This is all the Register mentions of him, so that we cannot
say whether he was buried in the church or churchyard; nor is

---

* The original Register of this Parish, which has been copied into the present
one, bears date from October the 24th, 1538.

there now any other memorial of him, except the tradition in the family, and some little marks of the place where his house stood. The story my lord told me was thus:—

" ' When Sir Thomas Moyle built that house (that is, Eastwell Place), he observed his chief bricklayer, whenever he left off work, retired with a book. Sir Thomas had a curiosity to know what book the man read, but was some time before he could discover it; he still putting the book up if anyone came towards him. However, at last Sir Thomas surprised him,* and snatched the book from him; and looking into it, he found it to be Latin. Hereupon he examined him; and finding he pretty well understood that language, he inquired how he came by his learning. Hereupon, the man told him, as he had been a good master to him, he would venture to trust him with a secret he had never before revealed to anyone. He then informed him† that he was boarded with a Latin schoolmaster, without knowing who his parents were, till he was fifteen or sixteen years old; only a gentleman (who took occasion to acquaint him he was no relation to him) came once a quarter and paid for his board, and took care to see that he wanted nothing; and one day this gentleman took him and carried him to a fine great house, where he passed through several stately rooms, in one of which he left him, bidding him stay there. Then a man, finely dressed, with a star and garter, came to him, asked him some questions, talked kindly to him, and gave him some money.‡ Then the fore-mentioned gentleman returned and conducted him back to his school.§ Some time after, the same gentleman came to him again, with a horse and proper accoutrements, and told him he must take a journey with him into the country. They went into Leicestershire, and came to Bosworth field, and he was carried to King Richard the Third's tent. The king embraced him, and told him he was his son; ' but, child,' says he, ' to-morrow I must fight for my crown; and assure yourself, if I lose that, I will lose my life also: but I hope to preserve both. Do you stand in such a place (directing him to a particular place), where

---

VARIATIONS.

* " ' Mr. Peck says, he saw another account, the most material difference of which he gives in a note as follows:—' The knight once coming into his room while he lay asleep with his hand on the table, he saw a book lying by him.' "

† " ' I was,' he said, ' brought up at my nurse's house, whom I took for my mother, until I was seven years old. Then a gentleman, whom I did not know, took me from thence, and carried me to a private school in Leicestershire.' "

‡ " ' Who examined me very narrowly, and felt my limbs and joints, and gave me ten pieces of gold—viz., crown gold, which was the current money then, and worth ten shillings a piece.' "

§ " ' About a year after, he sent for me again, looked very kindly on me, and gave me the same sum.' "

you may see the battle, out of danger; and when I have gained the victory, come to me, and I will then own you to be mine, and take care of you.   But if I should be so unfortunate as to lose the battle, then shift as well as you can; and take care to let nobody know that I am your father, for no mercy will be shown to anyone so nearly related to me.'   Then the king gave him a purse of gold, and dismissed him.*

"'He followed the king's directions; and when he saw the battle lost and the king killed, he hastened to London, sold his horse and fine clothes, and, the better to conceal himself from suspicion of being son to a king, and that he might have means to live by his honest labour, he put himself apprentice to a bricklayer.†   But having a competent skill in the Latin tongue, he was unwilling to lose it; and having an inclination also to reading, and having no delight in the conversation of those he was obliged to work with, he generally spent all the time he had to spare in reading by himself.   Sir Thomas said, 'You are now old, and almost past your labour; I will give you the running of my kitchen, as long as you live.'   He answered, 'Sir, you have a numerous family.   I have been used to live retired; give me leave to build a house of one room for myself, in such a field, and there, with your good leave, I will live and die; and if you have any work that I can do for you, I shall be ready to serve you.'   Sir Thomas granted his request: he built his house, and there continued to his death.   I suppose, though my lord did not mention it, that he went to eat in the family, and then returned to his hut. My lord said there was no park at that time; but when the park was made, that house was taken into it, and continued standing until his (my lord's) father pulled it down.   'But,' said my lord, 'I would as soon have pulled down this house (meaning Eastwell Place).'"

BRAYLEY'S BEAUTIES OF ENGLAND AND WALES,
vol. viii. (Kent).

VARIATIONS.

* "'He asked me whether we heard any news at our school?   I said, the news was, the Earl of Richmond was landed, and marched against King Richard. He said he was on the king's side, and a friend to Richard.   Then he gave me twelve hundred of the same pieces, and said, 'If King Richard gets the better in the contest, you may then come to court, and you shall be provided for; but if he is worsted or killed, take this money, and go to London, and provide for yourself as you can.'"

† "'After the battle was over, I set out, accordingly, for London; and just as I came to Leicester, I saw a dead body brought to town upon a horse, and, upon steadfastly looking upon it, I found it to be my father.   I then went forward to town; and my genius leading me to architecture, as I was looking on a fine house that was building there, one of the workmen employed me about something; and, finding me very handy, took me to his house, and taught me the trade which now occupies me.'"

[40] *As Barnard's or as Crosby Hall have been.*

Barnard's Castle, and Crósby Place—the residences in London of the Duke of Gloucester, afterwards King Richard the Third.

[41] *Between us lives, alas ! no longer one.*

The Prince of Wales, son of King Richard the Third, had died in 1484, the year before the battle of Bosworth Field.

[42] *This seal and high commission are thine own;*
They give thee Calais, Guisnes, with our domain
In France.

"Richard left one natural son, a minor, whom he had appointed Governor of Calais, Guisnes, and all the marches of Picardy, belonging to the crown of England."

SMOLLETT.

[43] *With Radcliff for thy guide.*

"Sir Richard Radcliff, killed on Richard's side, in the battle of Bosworth Field.

[44] *Gave and returned a patriarchal prayer,*
Like him of Bethlehem.

"And, behold! Boaz came from Bethlehem, and said to the reapers, 'The Lord be with you!' and they answered him, 'The Lord bless thee!'"

BOOK OF RUTH, Chap. 2.

[45] *That well he merited his valour's fame.*

"He (Richard the Third) possessed such courage as no danger could dismay."

SMOLLETT.

[46] *Who spared Lord Stanley's blood, his own the cost.*

"Lord Stanley, who quitted Atherstone, took post in a piece of ground fronting the interval between the two armies; and his brother, at the head of two thousand men, stood facing him on the other side. Richard, suspecting Stanley's design, ordered him to join his army; and, receiving an equivocal answer, would have put his son to death, had he not been diverted from his purpose by the remonstrances of his generals, who observed that such a sacrifice could be of no advantage to the royal cause, but would infallibly provoke Stanley and his brother to join the foe, though perhaps their intention was to remain neuter, and declare for the victor.

"Richard was persuaded by this representation; but he committed a fatal error in leaving the two brothers at liberty to act as they should think proper. His army being equal in number to that of Richmond and the Stanleys, when joined together, he might have posted two bodies opposite to the brothers, with orders to attack them if they should attempt to join the enemy; while he himself, with the remainder, might have given battle to Henry."

SMOLLETT.

[47] *Which I would spare.*

"For life, I prize it,
As I would grief, which I would spare."

SHAKSPEARE (Hermione: Winter's Tale).

[48] *The honeybee and martlet loved the spot.*

"This guest of summer,
The temple-hunting martlet, does approve,
By his loved masonry, that the heaven's breath
Smells wooingly here: no jetty, frieze, buttress,
Nor coigne of vantage, but this bird hath made
His pendent bed and procreant cradle. Where they
Most breed and haunt, I have observed the air
Is delicate."

SHAKSPEARE (Macbeth).

[49] *Until fourscore had sped.*

Richard Plantagenet died 1550, anno 4, King Edward the Sixth: aged, as is supposed, about eighty-one. King Edward the Sixth died 1553.

[50] *The tomb, accounted his, has lost its shield,*
And stands without a title.

"Whatever may be the truth as to the traditionary tale, the tomb itself seems of an earlier period: it has been inlaid with brasses, which are now gone."

BRAYLEY'S BEAUTIES OF ENGLAND AND WALES.

[51] *Men forget*
His place.

The house in which Richard Plantagenet lived and died was pulled down by Heneage, Earl of Winchelsea, who died in 1689.

Light.

PART I.

How beautiful is light!
The primal gift, prepared for man
Ere ordinance of earth began:
Which He, whose Spirit moved upon the flood,
Commanding it arise
Before he made the skies,
Beheld, and the Creator called it good.
Then, alternation sweet of night
Attempered its ethereal ray,
And evening and morning were a day.

How beautiful was light, as first it shone
Amid the firmamental throne!
The waters, parted from the waters, saw
And owned alike the good Creator's law.
The second evening and morning were,
And angels breathed ambrosial atmosphere!
How beautiful was light,
In ordered radiance bright!

Then came a voice—the nether waters heard:
Dry land beneath the firmament appeared;
Receiving in its hour of birth,
Distinct from sea, the name of earth.

How beautiful the light that wandered o'er
The first wave, rippling on the trackless shore,
  And golden sand, and rocky mound
  That chafed it into deeper sound,
  Headland and shallow far away
  Empurpled by the nascent ray!
Far, far away, the bright creation ranged:
Its lovely plains and valleys interchanged
With everlasting hills and heights were seen,
Their summits mingling in the blue serene,
In all profusion and variety,
Beneath the fragrance of the morning sky.
Perchance, that orient breath of perfume called
The blush of chrysolite and emerald
    From ev'ry dale and hill;
   And, when their harmonies awoke,
    New forms of herb and foliage broke
   From germs expanding still;
And thousand odours, as they sprang, revealed
That Heaven clothed the lilies of the field.
Nor these alone; still, still attraction stirred;
  And, with its influence, began
    The fruit tree, yielding fruit, which bore
    Within itself the bounteous store
  Of sustenance designed for man;
And evening and morning were the third.

    Then, glorious orb of day!
     Thy sign in heav'n was seen;
    And thine, soft lunar ray,
     In nightly course serene!
Then, myriad galaxies of moving spheres,
For signs, for seasons, and for days and years,
  Diffusing in the depth and height
  The beauty and the power of light.

A people, to be born, will trace
Their empires in the realms of space;
How differing in glory know,
And what their influence below:
The central fire—the softer reign
Of crescent, swelling monthly to an orb—
The courses of the starry train—
The mists which erring meteors absorb—
And advocate, in time, for these,
Attractions, cycles, and degrees.
But happier who shall impart—
Holy and humble men of heart—
To those who listen while they gaze,
In wonder, gratitude, and praise,
How stood the sun on Gibeon's height,
And, moon! in valley thou of Ajalon,
Till Israel had ceased to smite,
And sin-avenging victory was won;
Because the Power who made their tribes his choice
Had listened to a mortal warrior's voice.

Up Tabor's steep ascent,
Ten thousand at her feet,
The matron ruler went.
Had Sisera to meet
No weapons of a foe
Save javelin and bow?
O contest keen and hard!
'Twas then from heaven they warred;
The stars against him in their courses fought,
Until his final overthrow was wrought.

And, in the fulness of the time,
Shall sages leave their eastern clime,
Obedient in faith and hope
To that celestial horoscope
Which shows the star of Bethlehem!

What is the long and arid path,
  The lightning's or tornado's wrath,
    Vigil, and fast, and toil, to them?
So, Heaven-directed, they attain the throne
Of Him whose light upon their valleys shone;
And myrrh, and gold, and frankincense supply,
Their gifts to Victim, King, and Deity.

But, when the newborn fires in heaven beamed,
Transgression to be punished or redeemed
Was none, nor any sorrow to alloy
The perfect transport of celestial joy
Which hailed the fourth return of orient light,
And sang its inclination into night;
  The morning stars in melody
  Concerting with the angelic cry.

Almighty power was moving in the wind,
  And deep within the bosom of the waves,
Which brought new creatures forth, of every kind,
  To skim their surface or possess their caves:
  While, far aloof, on lightsome wing,
  The feathered tribes were gathering.
  They joyed to dip in ocean's dew
  Their plumes of many coloured hue,
    And poise them in the sky;
  And from the choir, then first essayed,
  Arose the voice which nature bade,
    Or strain of melody:
And on the fairy forms and music spell,
Another day, the fifth, beamed forth and fell.

  Revived again the morn,
  And nobler tribes were born,
By love divine commanded to suspire;
The things that creep, or move in airy gyre—

Four-footed race, that batten in the mead,
Or on the browses of the mountains feed,
Or in the desert stretch their mighty length.
Endowed with grace, docility, and strength,
They move, the female to the male assigned:
Their throats dilate, their voices swell the wind,
    The lieges of the world below.

    And who is their appointed king?
    To whom shall the Creator bring
    Their tribes, and prompt him to bestow,
    In eloquence of human speech,
    A name perpetual for each?
He comes, the last—he comes, ordained to prove
A miracle of mercy and of love :
A monarch over other kinds to reign,
    With majesty and honour crowned,
And little lower than the radiant train
    Whose alleluias hymn around.
Whom, after, from their common father born,
Shall grace and comeliness like his adorn,
As risen first from his Creator's hand,
In form and mind accomplished to command?
    The Lord of Life, who came
      Pitying our miseries,
    Assumed his mortal frame
      In less imperial guise,
    Obedient to law for man.
    His blessed pilgrimage began
    In infancy—attained to youth
    With meek advance in grace and truth,
And impress of a spotless prime alone:
The indwelling deity revealed to none,
Until the glory rested on his head,
With attestation from the Highest, shed

O'er Jordan's wave of light;
And from the mountain height
The lawgiver and prophet passed away
Before a vision of supremer ray,
And fell again, upon the chosen ear,
Acclaim of love, and new command to hear.

Then, as the sovereign assumed his state
  O'er all the tribes of ocean, earth, and air,
And held of Heaven his appointed mate—
  Pure as she was, and meek, and brightly fair
Above all future daughters of their line—[1]
Creation had fulfilled the word divine.
The sixth of days was sinking in the west,
And heralded a morn of sabbath rest.

  The mother holds in her embrace
  Her sleeping child, and bends to trace,
In that meek image of angelic dawn,
Lapped on the pillow whence its life is drawn,
The lineaments her own, and his, above
Her own admired—in ecstasy of love.
Joyous of youth and hope, the vows are paid:
The lover gazes on the beauteous maid,
  About to be his bride;
And each, from look of other gathering
Expression such as truth and virtue bring,
  Forgets the world beside.
The pious, at his own accomplished plan
By faith divine, for benefit of man,
  Which Heaven has vouchsafed to bless,
  Smiles in assurance of success.
But fond maternal look, and happy glow
Of joy and hope upon the lovers' brow,
And aspect his that faithfully reveals
His holy triumph and the joy he feels—

E'en that wherewith, elate and unsubdued,
The saint anticipates beatitude—
Were all unlike and little to compare
With theirs, unconscious of sin and care,
Who saw the seventh morn serenely rise,
And held its services in Paradise.
Their temple was the horizon-circled shade,
By skill of architect divine arrayed
In forms of loveliness, and thousand dyes
Emitting incense to the clear blue skies.
How beautiful the light that shed its rays,
Through each interstice, o'er the verdant maze
Enriched with floral tracery! that fell
Upon the waters, silent in their cell,
    Save that they visited the bowers,
    And gushed in rills round Eden's flowers!
Not yet disparted on their fourfold way,[2]
O'er gold and gems of Havilah to flow;
To compass Ethiopia's arid brow,
Or eastward in Assyrian valleys stray—
As Pison and as Gihon known to glide,
Hiddekel, and Euphrates' noble tide.
The choir was of an universal voice,
United in new being to rejoice—
The rite, of adoration more than prayer,
For none in sorrow or in need were there;
    And walked with them the Almighty King,
    Sole object of their worshipping.

There is another sabbath men will keep,
    When centuries are o'er,
And hushed the fountains of the mighty deep,
    Engulphing earth no more.
How beautiful, the light that shall be born [5]
In arching radiance on that hallowed morn!

When, first, refracted in the drops
    The pearly clouds diffuse,
It falls upon the mountain tops
    In its prismatic hues,
A double token of the peace assigned
By covenant of Heaven to mankind.

  From Ararat; their restingplace,
  Descend the patriarchal race.
  The newly verdant earth supplies
  An altar for their sacrifice.
  The chosen of the ransomed bleed,
    In more than solemn rite,
  Before their tribes to covert speed,
    Or wing again their flight;
  And there is witness of the bow
  That He, who bade, accepts the vow—
  That, while the powers of earth remain,
  No flood shall deluge it again,
  But harvest to the time of seed,
    And cold to genial ray,
  Summer to winter, shall succeed,
    Nor cease the night and day.

How mournfully one sabbath vigil passed!
To some, most sorrowful, perhaps their last!
  How sad its solitary rite!
  How heavily the morrow's light
Began to dawn upon their pious care,
  When, issuing forth, the weepers bore
  Ointment and spice, the precious store
It was their faithful office to prepare!
The darkness supernatural had passed—
  Quaking of earth no more was felt:
They trod the guilty capital in haste,
  And at the palm-bowered fissure knelt.

Oh, who shall roll away the stone?
Fear not, ye faithful! it is gone!
  Just at the dawn of light,
  In archangelic might,
A minister descended, to disclose
To his confounded and distracted foes
  An empty sepulchre.
  Behold, He is not there!
And ye, rejoice, O ransomed! at the dawn
  Of holy day, appointed to begin
When his transcendent mercy had withdrawn
  The rule, and power, and punishment of sin.
Henceforth your Sabbaths shall no more be kept
  Upon the seventh, but the first of days.
Not as among the hours when Jesus slept,
  But seasons of his all-reviving rays;
Wherein your adoration shall record
That he has both created and restored.

PART II.

THERE is a borrowed light,
Around the Augustan city's dome,
That mocks the shade of night—
Thy yearly ceremonial, Rome![1]
And who, with mind unmoved, surveys
That hemisphere of lucid rays;
And each incurved and shapely line
Of coruscations, that define
The double length of colonnade,
Contrasted with its inmost shade—
The radiance diffused that fills
The valleys of her seven hills—
And marks her yellow river flow,[2]
Incarnadined by crimson glow?
Or who, within that awful fane,
The illumination of the cross?[3]
While sweeps below the pompous train,
And croziers shake and censers toss,
And things that genius conceived,
And art unparagoned achieved,
In excellence, are there—

The tessellated and the sculptured stone,
The pictured tablet and the molten throne,
   The princely sepulchre!
  Oh, can such forms as men create
  Suspire, and move, and arbitrate?
  Or, is it an illusive spell
  That mocks reality so well—
Unseals the sources of delight and woe,
And bids the soul with admiration glow?
  And, see! the multitude arise,
  And throng the Sistine Galleries;[4]
  The solemn tapers one by one
  Expiring, till the last is gone,
  Amid the sound so deep and faint
    Of penitential woe,
  It seems an universal plaint
    For sin and shame below—
A supplication of our race combined
For Heaven's mercy upon lost mankind;
  Or wailing from the lips of those
  Whose final aspirations close,
  While angel ministers control
  The struggles of the parting soul!
Such is the ritual which some sincere
Among Italian votaries revere.
  The sense is rapt, the taste refined,
  Not sanctified the mind.

 Oh, who is he that would areed
Observance of a simpler creed?
With him behold the light awake
O'er dewy mead and spangled brake;
The shadow of the verdant hill,
Deep and prolonged, decreasing still,

The while assumes his way
The golden orb of day!
What blazonry the sunbeam throws
Among the fragrant linden rows,
Beside the streamlet that distils
And gurgles in its many rills,
Now welling forth, and now unseen,
And but revealed by livelier green.
The path by which young troops retire
Is verging to the village spire;
 And, hark! the church bells sound
  A warning to prepare
  Betimes for morning prayer,
 While all is still around!
Oh, there is light upon each youthful brow!
Light in the eye, and in the ruddy glow
Of cheek and lip! They speed, alert and gay,
Conning their Sabbath lesson by the way.

But now the hour preceding noon is near
A quicker summons strikes the watchful ear.
 The village church is dight
 For solemn simple rite;
And, hasting, in observance meet,
With willing but unequal feet,
There blooming youth and tranquil age
Complete their Sunday pilgrimage:
Master and servant, friend and friend,
Their holy purpose one, attend.
The pastor on their duteous ranks
Bestows his smile—receives the thanks
 That eyes of silent friends convey.
His venerable aspect cleared,
His aspiration breathed unheard
 Begins the monitory lay,

" Awake, my soul! and with the sun
Thy daily course of duty run."
Kind offices on him devolve.
He will exhort, confess, absolve;
Will lead the chant, and, glowing, raise
The psalm of prophecy and praise;
    Unseal the book inspired
Of covenants divine; precede
In meek profession of the creed,
    By truth eternal fired.
His supplication will inspire the train
    Of kneeling listeners around
To deprecate all earthly sin and stain—
    In full petition to abound
For all that may awaken or improve
Submission heavenly, and brother love.
Their thanksgivings shall with his own unite,
    Their meek appeal for pardon and for grace
    Meet his recital from the holiest place.
His preaching and his blessing close the rite.

    How sweetly wanes the light on those
    Who seek their undisturbed repose,
      Their Sabbath duties paid;
    The while, a calm and happy throng,
    They go the russet path along,
      And through the yellow glade!
The moon ascends.   How awfully serene
Her influence upon the twilight scene!
    A glow like dayspring seems ' invest
    The distant promontory's crest.
      Above, beneath, around,
        A sapphire hue absorbs
      The sky, and sea, and ground—
        That, spangled with its orbs;

These, visited by lunar ray,
Which lights perchance some tree and bay.
　But chiefly lustre falls
　Upon those hallowed walls—
An ample breadth, all pale and pure,
Save that each shaft and curvature,
And ev'ry spire's ascending height,
Are silvery with fairer light—
　Amid a depth of shade
　Which sight cannot pervade.

Now, haste and view the clouds expand,
　And fainter gleam their fires,
While, veering over mountain land,
　The hurricane retires.
Afar, their airy billows fill
The streams of rain, descending still,
And distant echoings reveal
The thunder's last emitted peal.
Light has a glorious office now
Upon that wild and stormy brow,
　Which changes like the cheek
　Of one about to speak,
Whose heart with rival furies burns,
That fire, subdue, and awe, by turns.
A moment, and its front is blue,
　With depth of amarantine shade
Which thousand rills of diamond hue
　From rifts of every cone pervade,
　　Fretting the lake below:
And then, the wave, and rock, and air,
Revive, with humid lustre fair,
　　And parting western glow.
Why sets the sun upon that ruined pile
With fairer seeming than his wonted smile—

Some bartisan, or tower, or wall,
Disclosed at ev'ry interval;
 While burnished light, with warmer glow,
 Divides the portal gloom below?
Why seem, beneath Italian sky,
 With yellow front and azure cleft,
The mountain forms more bright to lie,
 Almost of him bereft?
Declining power! his beams are shorn
Of all the keenness of the morn.
He wants the noontide glory, now,
 Wherewith he warmed the mead,
When gushed the vine juice in its flow
 Beneath the rustic tread.
 Why seems his later time
 More glorious than his prime?
It is that shadows of the mountain length
 Spread eastward over half the land,
Contrasting, in their strange unreal strength,
 With hues that on their verge expand;
 While darkness overpowers
 The vale and woodland bowers.

Oh, if it be delightful to survey
The lights and shadows of the setting day,
The variations of the stormy sky,
The magic hues of moonlight scenery,
 The glow of morn and eve—
 What joy must heart receive
 From intellectual light,
 With nobler lustre bright,
 By Heaven ceded to the span
 Sublime, insatiate, of man?
 'Tis his to soar with angel power,
 While natures less exalted cower.

The light, to lower creatures dim,
Is pure and palpable to him:
The visions of his mind unfold
Bright rays of genius, dropping gold.
  He breathes poetic fire,
  And animates the lyre:
His words descend like morning dew,
To fantasy and nature true:
  How copious the store!
They may be many as the leaves
  That drift before the autumnal wind,
Which earth upon her lap receives,
  In all fantastic shapes combined—
Ten thousand, and yet more!

  If intellectual ray
  Itself be brighter day,
What is the moral mirror, from the brink
Unstained of which, astonied, ever shrink
  All natures mean, and vile, and base,
  And virtue parts with brighter grace?
The light by which are seen ' arise
All mutual humanities—
  The sources, first essayed
  For sympathy, for aid;
Then welling from their salutary springs
For brave, and noble, and heroic things!
  Such rays have rested, bright
  In uncreated light,
Upon the battlefield where patriots bled;
Have beamed around the self-devoted head;
Have glorified the chief's and freeman's meed,
Whether to triumph or to die decreed.

  Such was the lustre brightening
  Around the Spartans and their king [5]

Who rose to meet the Persian host!
  Albeit the devoted few,
  Departing from their altars, knew
    The alternative of hope was lost,
Yet was their mien unchanged—their aspect bright,
As if appointed to some festal rite.
They marched—they left on that disastrous strand,
The war-worn relics of their patriot band,
Three hundred lives—how dearly sold! for those
Unnumbered of the mightiest of their foes ;
And, not unsung by sacred bard,[6] the gain
Of sweet memorial, ever to remain,
While valour holds its virtuous renown,
And piety transcends the victor's crown.

  Submit, fair heritage of France![7]
  Our banners on thy breezes dance,
    Our navy sweeps thy shore.
The plume of Cressy flaunts upon the brow
Of him who hastens to thine overthrow,
    And hope of aid is o'er!
  To others chivalrous and free,
  Edward is stern and proud to thee.
  Within thy long-beleagured gates
  The withering of famine waits:
    The portals but unclose
  To proffer an ejected train,
  Whom friends no longer can sustain,
    To mercy of their foes.
  Yet, there is ray of moral light
  That cheers the darkness of thy night!
  Six, self-devoted, of thy best—
  Such is the conqueror's behest—
  Are prostrated before his throne,
  Haltered and barefoot, to atone

For all who dared withstand
The invader of their land.
Alas! and shall their noble blood be shed?
So bids the monarch, and averts his head;
   So wills not one who scanned
   The brave devoted band
  With feminine and queenly ruth—
    The nearest to his throne and grace,
    The mother of his royal race,
Then owning one more promise of her truth.
Philippa sues : extinct is royal ire—
Its victims, pardoned and caressed, retire.

  Such was illumination thine, [8]
  O daughter of imperial line!
    And how serene the ray
    It shed, that solemn day,
When, confident in thine undaunted mind—
Thy cause, thy right, to Power on high consigned—
Upon the regal mount thy guidance held
The matchless courser, proud to be compelled,
   And waved to heaven's points thy hand,
   The sabre of supreme command.
How well St. Stephen's crown and robe became [9]
Thy queenly bearing, and thy peerless frame!
   How well, when both were laid aside,
 The tresses, spreading o'er thy neck of snow—
Thy colour, heightened by the summer glow—
    Adorned thy beauty's pride!
   A ray of purer light was shed [10]
   Around thy dedicated head,
  When, sore beset, but unsubdued,
    And ever undismayed,
  Thy matron glance heroic viewed
    Hungarian power arrayed,

And only softened at the face
Before thee laid in infant grace.
About the mother and her son
Pressed noble hearts, by duty won,
And hands that half unsheathed their swords—
And lips of men devoted, murmuring
Implicit homage in their solemn words,
" We live, we vow to die, for thee, our king !"
O grateful heart! forbear,
Repress the rising tear.

PART III.

IF moral light, with mental power combined,
Have influence so noble on mankind—
Whither, oh, whither, may our aim extend,
By purer motive led to higher end,
If only the supremer light of grace
Above the lights of nature hold its place?

To subjugate, to triumph, to compel,
    Is all ambition of a master mind;
Perchance, to poise the mighty balance well,
    And, while it governs, benefit mankind.
Perchance, 'tis genius that bids explore
Systems and laws of intellectual lore;
To nature's highest principles ascends,
And to the power of its bidding bends
        The moral and the will,
        Its scope expanding still.
But all that fond humanity attains
Is circled by indissoluble chains;
The mystery of future circumvents
Hopes, fears, anticipations, and intents—
Contingencies, on which man reckons most,
By vacillation or mischance are lost—
The final hour dissolves the nearest ties—
And, with its instrument, the project dies—
As bubbles, by the buoyant air compelled,
Ascend, and burst, and are no more beheld.

Was not the victor's cheek with tears imbued [1]
Because he wanted worlds to be subdued?
Was not the wisest heathen fain' confess [2]
That all he knew was, his own nothingness?

But all, however arduous and bright,
Accedes to him whose heart is set aright;
And all is possible to him who rests,
In faith, on everlasting interests;
And what abases him whose heart is stayed,
Not on his own, but on almighty aid?
His, one ambition—to possess his soul
In truth, obedience, and self control;
His mortal joys and sorrows to refer
Alike to one eternal arbiter—
Impart his measure of celestial grace,
In pity, counsel, aid, to all his race!
Pure are his precepts, eloquent his song,
    Melodious his lyre;
To those the strains of Paradise belong,
    To these the seraph fire.
  How beautiful, the light he hath,
  Illuminating all his path!
  The mists of error, dense and pale—
    The depths that intervene,
  Along the sublunary vale,
    His path and home between—
  The sluggish waters of despond
  That mask the brighter shore beyond—
The fortalice of doubt, which gaunt Despair
Holds, armed and wakeful, on his iron lair—
The shoals and quicksands of the fair defile
Where syren Pleasure lavishes her smile—
All are apparent by the light of grace
That glows, a beacon, from his restingplace;

                             M 2

And, lo! a monitor, whose words assure—
"This is the way : be steadfast and secure."

    Whose are that light and voice?
    O rescued man, rejoice!
  Both are of Him, before whose feet,
  With sorrow and repentance meet,
    Our common parents lay,
    In their transgression day—
Of Him who, when the forfeit to be paid,
Oh, deathful, irreversible! was said,
Foretold in theirs and in the tempter's ear,
The part it was his providence to bear
For restoration of their fallen line,
Their future victory and palm divine—
  Of Him, Jesurun's stay and shield,
  Descending, in his power revealed,
  With rite and ordinance to prove
  The chosen nation of his love :
What time the trumpet pealed exceeding loud,
And, in the darkness of the thundercloud,
And fire wherewith encircled Sinai burned,
Was supplication made and voice returned.

  And, when the day began to spring
  Of fallen man's illumining—
When purer than his sinless grace had been
Was in the life of one exemplar seen—
And when the things, appointed to be known
By them the Lord had chosen for his own,
  Had been delivered and believed,
  The treasure of his peace received—[3]
When all had been accomplished of his plan
That could be ministered on earth to man,

And, led as far as Bethany, they went
With minds prepared to meet the bright event—
Then were his hands, in act of parting, raised
To bless the men who worshipped while they gazed,
And on their hearts and memories impressed
The consummation of his high behest:
To tell—baptizing in the name divine
With water, his regeneration sign—
All that he had enjoined to be obeyed,
 To ev'ry age, in ev'ry clime,
Sure of his grace, his presence, and his aid,
  Until an end of time.
 And then the clouds of heaven bore
 His form, terrestrial no more,
  Ascending from their sight
  Into eternal light!
" Ye men of Galilee, why stand and view?"
 (Thus to the gazers spake angelic twain)
" The same that your uplifted eyes pursue,
 As ye have seen depart, shall come again!"
And what, until his coming, shall remove
His faithful people from his saving love?
 Shall tribulation, or distress,
 Oppression, famine, nakedness,
  Or peril, or the sword,
  Divide them from their Lord?
  No; neither life nor death,
  Nor things above, beneath,
 Present and in futurity,
Throne, principality, nor seraphim,
 Shall alienate the rich supply
Of grace from the Supreme, which is by him.

Yet shall this cheering monitory ray
Become effused in everlasting day—

Be numbered but in retrospect
Among the myriads elect:
As shepherds, in the radiance of noon,
Desire no more the paler light,
Softly descending from the autumnal moon,
Upon some purple mountain height;
From which, in faith and patience, they told
The gathered numbers of their sleeping fold—
Albeit such, abiding in the field
Of Bethlehem, had wondrous light revealed,
And heard angelic minstrelsy prolong
The joyful reconciliation song—
For light of grace shall be resolved in light
Unchangeable, and ever, ever bright!

    The Lion of his tribe, the Stem
    And righteous Branch of Bethlehem,
Has, by his single potency, revealed
The mystery, from the beginning sealed.
Celestial harps acclaim the Lamb that bled,
And odours from the golden vials shed. [4]

    Ten thousand times ten thousand raise,
      And thousand thousands own,
    In seraph euphony his praise,
      Receiving from the throne
The charactered and seven-shielded scroll
Which he alone is worthy to unrol.
    And who is there inspired to say,
      What prophet shall areed,
    The portion that has passed away,
      And what is to succeed?
Behold! the mystic rider of the horse,
    Armed with his bow and crowned a king,
Has issued forth in his resistless force,
    To conquer, and still conquering.
And, lo! the fatal ministers proceed
On fiery, on black, and death-pale steed,

To whom it is assigned
To disunite mankind—
To mete in double balances the grain,
  And not to hurt the wine and oil—
To give a quarter portion of the slain
To sword and hunger, death and savage spoil.
But still the sainted chivalry of light,
With titled brows, and palms, and vestures white,
Advance in their victorious array
Whithersoe'er their captain leads the way.
  And, when the seventh awful band
  Has yielded to the loosing hand,
As many warning trumpet tones have pealed,
And thunders uttered voices unrevealed;
And powers have sped, commissioned to distil
Each wrathful drop of the supremest ill;
All will be finished that decree sublime
Allots to fate, mortality, and time,
And earth and heaven, perished and restored,
Be kingdoms of an universal lord.

How beautiful, the perfect light
  Of that eternal day;
Subsiding never into night,
  Nor ever to decay!
Behold the seat of the beatified
  Descending from above,
In gracefulness and lustre like a bride
  Adorned to meet her love!
For He, by whose decree began
The former heritage of man—
Which, smitten for his sin, decayed,
  Until the lapse of time was o'er—
Has in redeeming mercy said,
  "Behold a world to change no more!"

And, if it be permitted to declare
  Things inconceivable and unconceived
By parables of all exceeding rare
  That man in estimation has received—
That city, with its paths, is golden all,
On which the beams of heaven's glory fall.
Its vast and lofty walls are jasper pure;
Each gate a pearl, which angels twelve secure—
  A tribe of Israel is told
  Inscribed on each revolving fold.
  Twelve its foundations : borne on each,
    In precious stones enshrined,
  Their names, the first ordained to preach
    Salvation to mankind.
It has no temple set apart for prayer,
For all alike is pure and holy there;
No sun nor moon that shall arise and shine,
For its illumination is divine.
    Open by night and day
    Its broad and perfect way;
And thither flow the glory and the pride,
Worship and blessing of the sanctified.
The river of the font of life descends
    In ever tideless wave;
Whithersoe'er the crystal water wends,
    Omnipotent to save.
Amid its current, and on either shore,
Bloom foliage and fruit, unfailing store—
  Forth of the tree of life they spring :
  Ambrosial, and varying
  At every season, these ; and those,
  For healing of all mortal woes.
  So, Jordan, thine autumnal flood,
    That overwelled its banks,
  Pellucid and untroubled stood
    Before the priestly ranks;

And they abided with the charge they bore,
Until the tribes had gained their destined shore—
Then raised, and piled upon the promised land,
The tokens of their triumph and command.
    Thus—emblem weak and faint!
    The Syrian leper's taint [5]
Departed, when, in better mind, he bent
Amid thy waters, seven times besprent.

What are the legions dwelling, ever bright,
Amid the cloudless glory of that light?
    Spirits are these which grace has sped,
    And love and mercy perfected.
    Prophets, and priests, and kings, among
    The angelic choir they raise the song,
And, in eternal adoration, fall
Before the Lamb, and Him the Lord of all.

    If those, affectionately loved,
    Ere from mortality removed,
Had borne some secret yearning of the breast—
Some doubt, or wish, or purpose, unconfessed—
Had less devotedly and fondly deemed
Of some, perchance, who were not what they seemed—
If some survivor felt that humbling thought,
' I cherished not, nor loved them, as I ought'—
    If fortitude and faith had veered
        As life had sped away;
    While deathly shadows spread, uncheered
        By some imagined ray—
All, all, is clear, and pure, and exquisite,
In that blest region where they reunite;
And nothing absent; nothing they forget,
Save error, disappointment, and regret.
    Perchance, men found in holy writ
    Rescripts transcending human wit;

In humble faith had pondered o'er
Some teaching that their Lord forbore—
  Some precept or reply
  Obscure, and marvelled why;
  But dimness is withdrawn
  From that eternal dawn:
The accounted worthy of the crown,
Know, even as themselves are known.

The present state is fallible to man—
Somewhat he neither can exceed nor scan:
The measure that his powers and wishes meet,
Is, like his faith and virtue, incomplete:
Visions serene and bright remotely pass
Among the shadows on the mental glass:
  But here are unrefrained delight
  In all things good, and pure, and bright—
Accessions of intelligence, that fill
A cycle glorious, expanding still;
  And ever, ever to increase
  In plenitude that shall not cease.
    O great and glorious day!
    O rapture of that ray!
  Waft, waft my soul on seraph wings
    To light's celestial springs—
    To beams that will pervade,
    Without decline or shade,
Perception, intellect, affections, joy,
Through all a never changing life's employ;
    Amid th' eternal song
Which spirits of the blest alone can raise,
    And angel choirs prolong,
In wonder, love, and gratitude, and praise.

  How beautiful, how bright,
  Is everlasting light!

NOTES.

PART I.

[1] *Fair*
Above all future daughters of their line.

" So, hand in hand, they passed—the loveliest pair
That ever since in love's embraces met:
Adam, the goodliest man of men since born
His sons; the fairest of her daughters, Eve."

MILTON; Par. Lost, book iv. line 321.

[2] *Not yet disparted on their fourfold way.*

" And a river went out of Eden, to water the garden; and from thence it was parted, and became into four heads.

" The name of the first is Pison; that is it which compasseth the whole land of Havilah, where there is gold;

" And the gold of that land is good: there is the bdellium, and the onyx stone.

" And the name of the second river is Gihon: the same is it that compasseth the whole land of Ethiopia.

" And the name of the third river is Hiddekel: that is it which goeth to the east of Assyria.   And the fourth river is Euphrates."

GEN. ii. 10–14.

[3] *How beautiful, the light that shall be born*
In arching radiance!

" The rainbow is exhibited in a rainy sky, opposite to the sun, by the refraction of his rays in drops of falling rain.   There is also a secondary bow, which is fainter, usually investing the former at some distance.

" Anton de Deminis first accounted for the rainbow, in 1611, by refraction and reflection of the sunbeams in spherical drops of water, which he confirmed by experiments made with glass globes, &c. full of water; wherein he was followed by Descartes, who improved upon his account: but the Newtonian doctrine of colours supplies and corrects their explications.

" Each rainbow is variegated with all the prismatic colours.   This is a necessary consequence of the different refrangibility of the rays, refracted and reflected in drops of falling rain. Sometimes more than two bows appear, as, in a very black cloud, we have observed a fourth, and a faint appearance of a fifth; but this happens rarely."

Dict. Arts and Sciences.

PART II.

[1] *Thy yearly ceremonial, Rome!*

" Easter Sunday, 1818.

" We have just witnessed one of the most brilliant spectacles in the world—the illumination of St. Peter's. As we passed the Ponte St. Angelo, the appearance of this immense magnificent church, glowing in its own brightness—the millions of lights reflected in the calm waters of the Tiber, and mingling with the last golden glow of evening, so as to make the whole building seem covered with burnished gold—had a most striking and magical effect. At length we arrived at the Piazza of St. Peter's. The gathering shades of night rendered the illumination every moment more brilliant.

" The whole of this immense church—its columns, capitals, cornices, and pediments—the beautiful swell of the lofty dome, towering into heaven, the ribs converging into one point at top, surmounted by the lantern of the church, and crowned by the cross—all were designed in lines of fire; and the vast sweep of the circling colonnades, in every rib, line, mould, cornice, and column, was resplendent with the same beautiful light. While we were gazing upon it, suddenly a bell chimed. On the cross of fire at the top waved a brilliant light, as if wielded by some celestial hand: and instantly ten thousand globes and stars of vivid fire seemed to roll spontaneously along the building, as if by magic; and, self-kindled, it blazed in a moment into one dazzling flood of glory."

Rome in the Nineteenth Century, Letter 77.

[2] *And marks her yellow river flow.*
" Vidimus flavum Tiberim."
Hor. lib. i., od. 2.

[3] *The illumination of the cross.*

" The effect of the blazing cross of fire, suspended from the dome above the confession, or tomb of St. Peter, was strikingly brilliant at night, when, at the conclusion of the Miserere, we descended into the church, the immense expanse of which was thoroughly illuminated with its resplendent brightness. It is covered with innumerable lamps, which have the effect of one blaze of fire."

ROME IN THE NINETEENTH CENTURY, Letter 73.

4 *And throng the Sistine Galleries.*

"The shadows of the evening had now closed in. After a deep and most impressive pause of silence, the solemn Miserere commenced; and never, by mortal ear, was heard a strain of such powerful, such heart-moving pathos. The accordant tones of a hundred human voices, and one which seemed more than human, ascended to heaven together for mercy to mankind—for pardon to a guilty and sinning world. It had nothing in it of this earth, nothing that breathed the ordinary feelings of our nature: it seemed as if every sense and power had been concentered into that plaintive expression of lamentation, of deep suffering, and supplication, which possessed the soul. It was the strain that disembodied spirits might have used, who had just passed the boundaries of death, and sought release from the mysterious weight of woe and the tremblings of mortal agony that they had suffered in the passage of the grave: it was the music of another state of being.

"It ceased. A priest, with a light, moved across the chapel, and carried a book to the officiating Cardinal, who read a few words in an awful and impressive tone. Then again the light disappeared, and the last, the most entrancing harmony, arose, in a strain that might have moved heaven itself—a deeper, more pathetic sound of lamentation, than mortal voice ever breathed. It was the music of Allegri; but the composition, however fine, is nothing without the voices who perform it here. It is only the singers of the Papal Chapel who can execute the Miserere. It has been tried by the best singers in Germany and totally failed of success. There is never any accompaniment, though at times the solemn swell of the softened organ seemed to blend with the voices.

"This music is more wonderful, and its effects more powerful, than anything I could have conceived. At its termination, some loud strokes that reverberated through the chapel, and are intended, I was told, to represent the vail of the temple being rent in twain, closed the service."

ROME IN THE NINETEENTH CENTURY, Letter 73.

5 *Around the Spartans and their king.*

Leonidas, first king of the Lacedemonians, famous for his courage and genius. He defended the pass of Thermopylæ, with only three hundred men, against the immense army of Xerxes, and died there with his soldiers; but they acquired immortal glory.

COLLIGNON'S LADVOCAT. BIOG. DIC., vol. 3.

[6] *And, not unsung by sacred bard.*

Vixere fortes ante Agamemnona
Multi: sed omnes illacrymabiles
Urgentur, ignotique longâ
Nocte, carent quia vate sacro.

HOR., CAR., lib. iv. od. 9.

See "LEONIDAS," an English Epic Poem, by Mr. Glover.

[7] *Submit, fair heritage of France!*

The garrison of Calais made a noble defence, under John de Vienne, who repulsed the besiegers in all their assaults. Edward, seeing no prospect of reducing it by force, resolved to starve them into submission. He received supplies of men and provision from England, and a strong fleet blocked up the harbour.

"John de Vienne, finding himself every day more and more hampered by a scarcity of provisions, turned out five hundred inhabitants from the town; and, Edward refusing to let them pass, they perished miserably, by cold and famine, between the city and the camp of the besiegers. The Governor of Calais desired to capitulate; but Edward insisted upon his surrendering at discretion, that the garrison and inhabitants might be ransomed or punished according to his will and pleasure. It was at length stipulated that six of the principal burghers should come forth, barefooted, with halters about their necks, and present the keys of the town and castle to Edward, who should punish them as he thought proper, and receive all the rest into mercy. Eustace de St. Pierre and five of his fellow citizens offered themselves voluntarily, as sacrifices for the rest of the inhabitants; and in all probability they would have suffered death, had not the generosity of their behaviour affected Queen Philippa, who interceded in their behalf and obtained their pardon. A.D. 1347."

Extracted from SMOLLETT'S HIST. ENG., vol. ii.

[8] *Such was illumination thine,*
O daughter of imperial line!

"On surveying this deplorable state of affairs, the cause of Maria Theresa appeared wholly desperate. Attacked by a formidable league, Vienna menaced with an instant siege, abandoned by all her allies, without treasure, a sufficient army, or able ministers, she seemed to have no other alternative than to receive the law from her most inveterate enemies. But this great princess now displayed a courage truly heroic; and, assisted by the subsidies of Great Britain, and animated by the zeal of her Hungarian subjects, rose superior to the storm.

"Soon after her accession she had conciliated the Hungarians; and, at her coronation, had received from her grateful subjects the warmest demonstrations of loyalty and affection. Mr. Robinson, who was an eyewitness of this ceremony, has well described the impression made on the surrounding multitude.

" ' The coronation on the 25th (June, 1741) was leste, magnificent, and well ordered. The Queen was all charm; she rode gallantly up the royal mount, and defied the four corners of the world with the drawn sabre in a manner to show that she had no occasion for that weapon to conquer all who saw her. The antiquated crown received new graces from her head; and the old tattered robe of St. Stephen became her as well as her own rich habit—if diamonds, pearls, and all sorts of precious stones can be called cloaths.

" ' Illam, quicquid agit, quoquo vestigia vertit,
Componit furtim, subsequiturque decor.'

" An air of delicacy, occasioned by her recent confinement, increased the personal attractions of this beautiful princess; but when she sat down to dine in public, she appeared still more engaging without her crown. The heat of the weather and the fatigues of the ceremony diffused an animated glow over her countenance, while her beautiful hair flowed in ringlets over her shoulders and bosom."

COXE'S HIST. OF THE HOUSE OF AUSTRIA, vol. ii. chap. 22.

9   *How well St. Stephen's crown and robe became*
Thy queenly beauty and thy peerless frame!

" By degrees, their manners (*i. e.*, of the Hungarians) took a more civilized turn; and especially when, in the latter part of the tenth century, their prince, Geysa, embraced the Christian religion.

" His son Stephen, in 997 become the first King of Hungary, completed the establishment of the Christian religion, erected bishoprics, abbeys, and churches, annexed Transylvania as a province to Hungary, and at his death was canonized."

Extracted from CRUTTWELL'S GAZETTEER.

10   *A ray of purer light was shed*
Around thy dedicated head.

" She felt that a people, ardent for liberty and distinguished by elevation of soul and energy of character, would indignantly reject the mandates of a powerful despot, but would shed their blood in support of a defenceless Queen, who, under the pressure of misfortune, appealed to them for succour.

" Having summoned the States of the Diet to the castle, she entered the hall, and ascended the tribune from whence the sovereign is accustomed to harangue the States. After an awful silence of a few minutes, the Chancellor detailed the distressed situation of their sovereign, and requested immediate assistance. Maria Theresa then came forward and addressed the Deputies in Latin.

" The youth, beauty, and extreme distress of Maria Theresa, who was then pregnant, made an instantaneous impression on the whole assembly. All the Deputies drew their sabres half out of the scabbard; and then, throwing them back as far as the hilt, exclaimed, 'We will consecrate our lives and arms; we will die for our king, Maria Theresa!' Affected with this effusion of zeal and loyalty, the Queen, who had hitherto preserved a calm and dignified deportment, burst into tears of joy and gratitude.

"A similar, and not less affecting scene, took place when the Deputies assembled before the throne to receive the oath of the Duke of Lorraine, who had been appointed co-Regent of the kingdom by the consent of the Diet. At the conclusion of the ceremony, Francis, waving his hand, exclaimed, 'My blood and life for the Queen and kingdom!' and at the same moment the Queen exhibited the infant Archduke to the view of the assembly. A cry of joy and exultation instantly burst forth; and the Deputies repeated their exclamations, 'We will die for the Queen and her family! We will die for Maria Theresa!'"

COXE'S HIST. OF THE HOUSE OF AUSTRIA, vol. ii. chap. 22.

PART III.

[1] *Was not the victor's cheek with tears imbued?*

Recorded of Alexander the Great.

[2] *Was not the wisest heathen fain' confess
That all he knew was, his own nothingness?*

"The oracle declared Socrates to be the wisest of all the Grecians. Socrates declared that he knew only one thing, which was, that he knew nothing."

COLLIGNON'S LADVOCAT. BIOG. DIC., vol. iv.

[3] *The treasure of his peace received.*

"He then leaves them the precious legacy of peace of mind, which he calls his peace, because it can only be obtained through him; which he gives not as the world gives, a gift but in name, no better than an ineffectual wish, whereas his is an actual grant."

MACBRIDE, LECTURES ON THE DIALESSARON, part vi. 126.

[4] *And odours from the golden vials shed.*

"Which are the prayers of saints." REV. V. 8.

[5] *The Syrian leper's taint.*

Naaman.

"Then went he down, and dipped himself seven times in Jordan, according to the saying of the man of God: and his flesh came again, like unto the flesh of a little child, and he was clean."

2 KINGS V. 14.

C. & E. Layton, Printers, 150, Fleet Street.

Lightning Source UK Ltd.
Milton Keynes UK
UKHW020334081118
331957UK00008B/468/P